the great scallop

and oyster cookbook

whitecap

This edition published in the U.S. and Canada
by Whitecap Books Ltd.
For more information, contact:
Whitecap Books
351 Lynn Avenue
North Vancouver
British Columbia
Canada, V7J 2C4

Publisher: Richard Carroll
Production Manager: Anthony Carroll
Designer: Vincent Wee
Creative Director: Paul Sims
Computer Graphics: Lucy Adams
Food Photography: Gary Smith
Food Stylist: Janet Lodge
Food for Photography: Louise Hockham, Katrina Cleary
Recipe Development: Ellen Argyriou, Janet Lodge, Lyn Carroll
Proof Reader: Fiona Brodribb
Editor of North American edition: Marial Shea

National Library of Canada Cataloguing in Publication Data

The great scallop and oyster cookbook / ed. Marial Shea ; recipe development, Ellen Argyriou, Janet Lodge, Lyn Carroll.

(Great seafood series)
Includes index.
ISBN 1-55285-539-2

1. Cookery (Shellfish) 2. Cookery (Oysters) I. Lodge, Janet. II. Argyriou, Ellen. III. Carroll, Lyn. IV. Shea, Marial. V. Series.

TX753.G74 2003   641.6'94   C2003-911236-5

First Edition Printed July 2002, reprinted 2003 and 2004. This edition printed April 2005.
Computer Typeset in Verdana, Trajan and Charcoal

Printed in China by Max Production Printing Ltd.

The publisher acknowledges the financial support of the Government of Canada through the Book Publishing
Industry Development Program for our publishing activities.

The publishers would like to thank Mr. John Mercer of the Marine &
Freshwater Resources Institute, Queenscliffe, Victoria for the
provision of photographs and information relating to scallop
aquaculture used in this book.

contents

INTRODUCTION

Scallops

Scallops are one of the most delectable foodstuffs to come from the sea. Scallops are so rich, sweet and tender that a little goes a long way. Beware, however, that some unscrupulous markets may try to palm off imposter seafood as scallops. Learn how to spot a true scallop, discover its history, and try some new recipes using this seafood treat.

A Little History

The word scallop comes from the Old French *escalope* meaning "shell," referring to the shell that houses the scallop. Scallops are mentioned in print as far back as 1280, when Marco Polo names scallops as one of the seafoods sold in the marketplace in Hangchow, China. Paris restaurateur Gustave Chatagnier featured a special scallop dish on his menu in 1936.

Probably the most famous scallop dish is Coquille Saint-Jacques. The word *coquille* means "shell" in French. The name of this dish has a religious history, but only in relation to the shell itself. The scallop shell was used as a badge of reverence and identification by pilgrims visiting the Spanish shrine of St. James (St. Jacques in French). The famous dish is made of a blend of scallops in a cream and butter sauce and is traditionally served in the beautiful shell of the scallop.

Types of Scallops

The scallop is a bivalve mollusk of the family Pectinidae. There are many varieties of scallop, ranging from the tiny, tender bay scallop to the larger, less tender deep sea scallop. The entire scallop within the shell is edible, but it is the white adductor muscle which hinges the two shells that is most commonly sold.

Oysters

Oysters are a very healthy food. They are easily digested, rich in vitamins and minerals. Oysters are highly adaptable and are currently being grown successfully in many locations.

Oysters are classified as shellfish, being covered with a shell, or invertebrates, having no backbone. They are further classified as mollusks, being of soft structure either partially or wholly enclosed in a hard shell that is largely of mineral composition.

Research shows that oysters are low in cholesterol and high in omega-3 oils, calcium, iron, zinc, copper and protein. All shellfish have some carbohydrate. Oysters contain 3–5 percent. Oysters also contain a somewhat higher percentage of calcium than other fish and meats, which are notably low in calcium. Oysters, clams and lobster contain more iodine than any other seafood. Few foods can compare to oysters in terms of their nutritional value.

Oysters may be purchased live in the shell, fresh or frozen shucked (removed from the shell), or canned. When alive, they have a tightly closed shell.

SCALLOP PREPARATION

Like all shellfish, scallops deteriorate quickly once out of the water, so they are usually sold shucked (shelled). When you buy them, check to make sure they have a sweet odor and a moist sheen. Scallops range in color from a light beige to a creamy pink. Beware of those that are stark white as they've likely been soaked in water to increase their weight for sale. Though the entire scallop, including the corals (roe), can be eaten, most scallops sold in North America consist of the adductor muscle that hinges the two shells together.

Refrigerate fresh scallops immediately and use them within a day or two. Frozen scallops are an excellent option, as they are widely available year-round. If you are catching your own scallops, put them on ice immediately, as the cold causes them to open up. In contrast, warm scallops will demonstrate quite clearly the meaning of the expression "to clam up"!

Opening Scallop Shells

Step 1: With the dark side of the scallop up and the hinge facing away from you, insert a knife blade or sharpened spoon between the top and bottom shells, inserting, from the right. Cut away the muscle at its attachment to the top shell. Remove the top shell and discard.

Step 2: Remove the dark innards by gently scraping from hinge to front with a spoon or scallop knife. The innards will peel cleanly from the muscle if you carefully scrape over the muscle from hinge to front, pinching the innards against the knife or spoon with your thumb as you pass over the cut surface of the muscle.

Step 3: Now simply scrape the scallop from the bottom shell. Some people prefer to leave the muscle attached.

OYSTER PREPARATION

Fresh oysters are available year-round, although for serving raw, they're at their best during fall and winter. Buy oysters from shops with a rapid turn-over to insure freshness, and select only those with tightly closed shells (or that snap shut when tapped).

Cover live oysters with a damp towel and refrigerate, larger shells down, for up to 3 days. You can also purchase shucked (shelled) oysters. Look for plump meat with uniform size, good color and fresh smell, packed in clear (not cloudy) oyster liquor. Use shucked oysters within 2 days. Oysters are also available canned in water or oyster liquor, frozen and smoked.

If you use technique rather than strength, oysters are easy to open. Hold the unopened oyster in a garden glove or tea towel to protect your hand from the rough shell. Open it with an oyster knife held in the other hand.

Step 1: Hold the oyster with the deep cut down and insert the tip of the oyster knife into the hinge. Twist to open the shell. Do not open oyster by attempting to insert the oyster knife into the front lip of the shell.

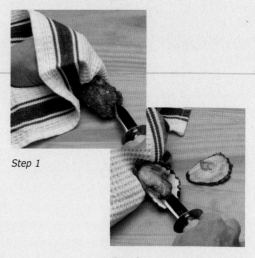

Step 1

Step 2

Step 2: Slide the oyster knife inside the upper shell to cut the muscle that attaches it to the shell. To serve, discard the upper part of shell, cut the muscle under the bottom half, then replace oyster into half shell.

SCALLOP FARMING

Growing scallops to market size usually takes 18 months to 2 years. First, a reliable source of scallop spat (spawn) is needed, either from the wild or from a hatchery.

Small holes are drilled in the "ears" of the scallop shells and they are suspended on a long line

Scallop Spat from the Wild

The natural settling behavior of scallop spat can be exploited by putting out collectors which simulate the conditions in which scallops normally set. Collectors are made by stuffing bundles of nylon fishing net into mesh onion bags. In the fall, when scallops usually spawn, these bags are anchored in the ocean a few meters above the bottom in a location where scallop spawn would naturally settle. The collectors are usually left in the water until the following summer, when the scallops will have grown to 1/3–1/2 inch (8–10mm) diameter, and will be large enough to handle.

Hatchery Culture

The alternative to collecting wild spat is to raise the spawn in a hatchery. Adult scallops are brought into the hatchery and conditioned by feeding them a mixture of several species of phyto-plankton. Part of the success of a hatchery lies in the quantity and quality of the phytoplankton. Water quality control is also important at all stages of the hatchery operation.

Eggs released by the females are captured on fine mesh screens and transferred to large tanks where the water is changed regularly and the tanks kept scrupulously clean. After hatching, the spawn are fed mixtures of cultured algae. They settle in for growth on rigid plastic sheeting or fiberglass panels suspended in the tanks.

Culture of Post-Settled Scallops

Once they have settled, the scallop spat may be held on screen-bottom trays. Warm water containing cultured algae is pumped to them. The most successful technique is one called an upweller. Screen-bottom trays or cylinders containing the spat are suspended in a tank into which water is pumped.

Intermediate Grow-out

At about one year old, when juvenile scallops are 1/4–1/2 inch (5–10mm) in diameter, they are ready for transfer to what is called intermediate grow-out, usually done in fine mesh lantern nets or pearl nets suspended on long lines deep enough in the water to be below the action of surface waves. Scallops do not like to be jiggled!

These long lines consist of polyethylene rope anchored firmly at each end, with floats and ballast weights to keep them below the wave action. The farmer's secret is to find a site where there is good water exchange, a supply of plankton and suitable temperatures.

Final Grow-out

Farmers have several options for the final grow-out. The so-called Chinese lantern net, or variants of it developed by individual growers, is commonly used. Scallops are loaded into the different levels and the nets are suspended in mid-water as before. As the scallops grow they are thinned into larger mesh nets. The secret is to have a mesh just small enough to prevent the escape of the scallops, and large enough to maximize water exchange.

An alternative is to pass loops or plastic toggles through small holes drilled in the "ears" of the scallop shell and suspend them from the long line. This can be done when the scallops are as small as 1¼ inches (3cm) in diameter, but the operation is delicate.

Tending the long lines is done either from a boat which hauls the line to the surface, or by divers who clip on or remove nets from the long line underwater.

Another option for farming scallops is to scatter them on the ocean bottom for harvest by conventional fishing techniques, or by divers. In this case growth to market size may take longer and mortality is higher, particularly among small scallops.

While there is variation in growth rate from site to site, and between individual scallops, suspended culture is still the more reliable method, growth being more rapid than when scallops are on the bottom, and loss to predators much reduced.

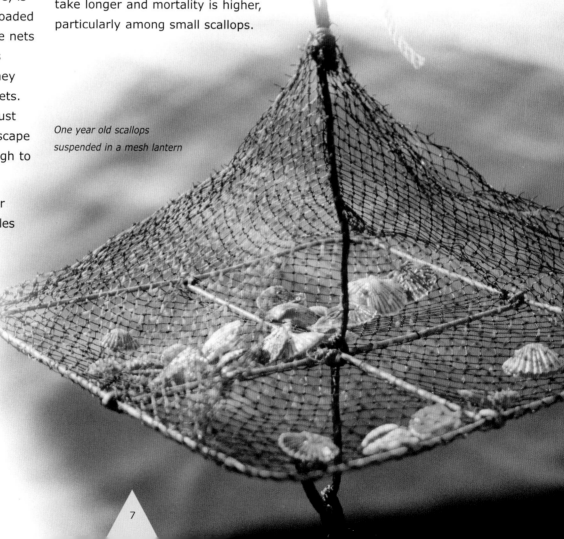

One year old scallops suspended in a mesh lantern

OYSTER FARMING

It takes at least 3 years of careful monitoring for an oyster to be ready for your table. At its best, modern oyster farming is a blend of tradition and technology.

Stick and Tray Culture

Stick and tray culture is the most common method of oyster farming. Stock depends on natural spatfall (spawn), which is collected on tarred and concreted hardwood sticks.

The sticks are placed in their catching areas attached to two horizontal runners. Twelve sticks are attached to the runners, then they are placed in pairs with the sticks both facing inwards, leaving a 1in/2.5cm gap between each stick. The gap is wide enough to allow the spat to grow strong, but narrow enough to stop predators.

At this time the sticks are separated into stacks with non-paired racks. This thins the oysters out, allowing more food per oyster. They are left like this for 7–8 months, when they are further separated into single sticks and left a further 6–12 months, after which they are harvested by hitting the stick with a hammer to shake off the oysters.

The oysters are then put loose in trays for about 9 months or more to fatten. From here they are purified, sorted and then sold. By the time they are sold the oysters will be 3–4 years old.

Single-Seed Culture

This involves using spat collected specially for the purpose of single-seed culture.

The spat are put in trays or cylinders. The trays allow growing space for the oyster to grow to a cup shape. In cylinders, the action of the tide rolls the cylinder around a pole, affecting the growth to produce a cupped oyster. If the oysters are grown for too long with this method then they will become soft shelled and undesirable.

Sub-Tidal Culture

Oysters grown with this type of culture generally grow faster than intertidally grown oysters because they spend all of their time underwater, meaning they can feed more often. Their condition also recovers more quickly after spawning than oysters grown intertidally.

Off-bottom Culture

In off-bottom culture, oysters are grown suspended on structures in the water between the surface and the bottom. The Japanese prefer using rafts. Another method uses PVC pipes glued together and capped to form floats 20–26 yards (18–24m) long. The pipes are used in pairs to support sticks or trays. The sticks can be submerged for 8–12 months, after which the oysters are knocked off and grown in trays.

Dredge Bed Culture

The operation is simple: a layer of oyster shells is deposited on hard, clean bottoms of estuaries; the spat then collects and grows on this and the oysters are harvested by systematically dredging the bottom with a small dredger about 1 yard (1m) wide.

APPETIZERS & SNACKS

Lemon and Herb Basted Scallops

INGREDIENTS

4 tablespoons/60mL butter, melted

2 tablespoons/25mL lemon juice

1 clove garlic, crushed

1 teaspoon/5mL fresh basil,
   finely chopped

1 teaspoon/5mL cilantro,
   finely chopped

1 teaspoon/5mL fresh mint,
   finely chopped

16oz/500g package frozen scallops

1 red onion, cut into wedges

1 red bell pepper, cut into triangles

wooden skewers

watercress

lemon wedges

METHOD

1. Combine the butter, lemon juice, garlic and herbs and set aside.

2. Thread scallops, onion and red bell pepper onto skewers and brush with the butter mixture.

3. Place the skewers onto a preheated grill plate turning once and brushing with butter mixture, until scallops are just cooked (approximately 5 minutes).

3. Serve garnished with watercress and lemon wedges.

Serves 6

Devilled Oysters

INGREDIENTS

12 small oysters, shucked

1 tablespoon/15mL red wine vinegar

1 teaspoon/5mL Worcestershire sauce

a few drops Tabasco sauce

2 tablespoons/25mL butter

1 shallot, finely chopped

1 clove garlic, crushed

2oz/50g piece pancetta
   or smoked bacon, finely chopped

1 cup/250mL fresh white breadcrumbs

2 tablespoons/25mL freshly grated
   Parmesan cheese

1 tablespoon/15mL fresh parsley, chopped

a little olive oil

salt and pepper

METHOD

1. Carefully strain the juices from the oysters into a bowl and stir in the vinegar, Worcestershire sauce and Tabasco sauce. Cut through the muscle that attaches the oyster to the deep half of the shell, but leave the oysters in the shell. Discard the other half of the shell.

2. Melt the butter in a small pan and fry the shallot and garlic for 5 minutes. Add the pancetta or bacon and stir-fry for a further 3–4 minutes until browned.

3. Add the breadcrumbs and pour in the oyster juice mixture. Boil until the liquid has nearly all evaporated. Remove from the heat and stir in the Parmesan and parsley and season to taste with salt and pepper. Leave to cool.

4. Arrange the oysters in a baking dish and top each one with the breadcrumb mixture. Drizzle over a little olive oil and cook under a preheated grill for 3–4 minutes until bubbling and golden. Serve at once.

Serves 6

LEMON AND HERB BASTED SCALLOPS

Scallop and Green Bean Terrine

INGREDIENTS

10oz/285g sea scallops, rinsed

1 tablespoon/15mL egg white, lightly beaten

1 teaspoon/5mL salt

1/4 teaspoon/2mL white pepper or to taste

1/8 teaspoon/1mL nutmeg

**1 1/2 cups/375mL green beans, trimmed
and cut into 1/4in/5mm pieces**

**2 tablespoons/25mL unsalted butter,
softened**

1 1/4 cups/300mL crème fraîche (see Note)

1/3 cup/75mL Parmesan cheese, grated

3/4 cup/75mL tomato coulis (see below)

Tomato Coulis

14oz/398mL can crushed tomatoes

1 onion, chopped

1 teaspoon/5mL butter

1 tablespoon/15mL crushed garlic

1/8 teaspoon/1mL dried sage

METHOD

1. In a food processor with a metal blade, puree the scallops with the egg white, salt, white pepper and nutmeg. Transfer the puree to a metal bowl and chill, covered, for 1 hour. In a saucepan, blanch the green beans in boiling salted water for 6 minutes. Drain.

2. Toss the beans with 1 tablespoon/15mL of the butter, season them with salt and white pepper to taste and set aside. Set the bowl of puree in a larger bowl of ice water. Beat in 1 cup/250mL of crème fraîche, 1/4 cup/50mL at a time, until it is incorporated and the mousse is fluffy.

3. Fold in the green beans and spoon the mousse into a buttered terrine. Place terrine in a baking pan and add enough hot water to reach 2/3 the way up the side of the terrine.

4. Bake, covered with a buttered sheet of wax paper and the lid or a double layer of foil, in a preheated 375°F/190°C oven for 45 minutes. Remove terrine from pan, remove lid and paper, and allow to cool for at least 30 minutes. Cut into 6 slices and arrange slices in a buttered gratin dish just large enough to hold them in one layer. Spread some of the remaining butter lightly over each slice and sprinkle with Parmesan cheese.

5. Bake in a preheated 400°F/200°C oven for 20–25 minutes, or until they are hot and puffed slightly. In a saucepan, combine the tomato coulis and the remaining crème fraîche. Heat the sauce over moderate heat, stirring, until it is heated through. Serve in a boat alongside the terrine.

Tomato Coulis

Sauté the onion and garlic over low heat until translucent. Add tomatoes and seasonings and simmer until most of the moisture has evaporated (should be the consistency of thick sauce).

Serves 6

Note: Crème fraîche is a lightly soured and thickened cream. Buy it at the grocery store or make your own by adding 1 teaspoon/5mL of buttermilk to 1 cup/250mL of heavy or whipping cream and let stand, covered, at warm room temperature about 12 hours. Keeps 1 week refrigerated.

Scallop Puffs

INGREDIENTS

9oz/250g sea scallops

1/4 cup/50mL/2fl oz mayonnaise

**1/4 cup/50mL freshly grated
  Gruyère cheese**

1/2 teaspoon/2mL Dijon-style mustard

1 teaspoon/5mL fresh lemon juice

**1 tablespoon/15mL finely chopped
  fresh parsley leaves**

salt and pepper

1 large egg white

**1 sheet puff pastry cut into 25 squares,
  2in x 2in/5cm x 5cm**

METHOD

1. Place the scallops in a saucepan with enough salted water to cover them completely. Bring the water to a simmer, and poach the scallops for 5 minutes. Drain the scallops well and cut them into 1/2in/1cm pieces.

2. In a bowl, whisk together the mayonnaise, Gruyére, mustard, lemon juice, parsley, and salt and pepper to taste. Add the scallops, and toss the mixture well. In a small bowl beat the egg white until it just holds stiff peaks and fold it into the scallop mixture, gently but thoroughly.

3. Place pastry squares that have been pricked with a fork onto a lined oven tray and bake at 200°F/100°C for 5 minutes, or until just turning golden.

4. Remove from oven, and place a heaped teaspoon of the scallop mixture onto each pastry square.

5. Place under a preheated grill, until the topping is bubbling and lightly golden, taking care not to burn the edges of the pastry.

Makes 25 hors d'oeuvres

Oysters in Tempura Batter

INGREDIENTS

20 oysters

Dipping Sauce
4 tablespoons/60mL dark soy sauce
4 tablespoons/60mL water
juice of 1 lime

sunflower oil for deep frying

Tempura Batter
1/2 cup/125mL cornstarch
1/2 cup/125mL all-purpose flour
small pinch salt
4 teaspoons/20mL toasted sesame seeds
3/4 cup/175mL/6fl oz ice cold soda water
lime wedges to serve

METHOD

1. Open all the oysters and pour off the liquid. Carefully cut the meat out of the deeper shells and retain the shells for serving.

2. Mix together the ingredients for the dipping sauce and pour into 4 dipping saucers.

3. Heat some oil for deep frying to 375°F/190°C.

4. Make the batter by sifting the cornstarch, flour and salt into a mixing bowl. Stir in the sesame seeds then stir in the ice cold soda water until just mixed. Add a little more water if it seems too thick. The batter should be very thin and almost transparent.

5. Dip the oysters, one at a time. Drop into the hot oil and fry for a minute until crisp and golden. Lift out and drain on paper towels.

6. Return the oysters to their shells and arrange on plates. Serve with lime wedges and dipping sauce.

Serves 4

Oyster Kebabs

INGREDIENTS

1 large jar fresh oysters (about 20)
all-purpose flour, salt and pepper
12 bamboo skewers (soaked in
    water for 30 minutes)
2 eggs, lightly beaten
2 cups/500mL fresh breadcrumbs
2 tablespoons/25mL parsley flakes
oil for deep frying

Seafood Sauce
4 tablespoons/60mL thickened cream
1 tablespoon/15mL tomato sauce
1 tablespoon/15mL lemon juice
2 tablespoons/25mL Worcestershire sauce
dash Tabasco sauce
1/2 teaspoon/2mL horseradish cream
pinch dry mustard
salt and cracked black peppercorns

METHOD

1. Drain oysters and toss in seasoned flour. Gently push oysters onto bamboo skewers.

2. Coat kebabs in beaten egg, then roll in breadcrumbs combined with parsley flakes.

3. Heat oil in frying pan. Fry quickly for about 1 minute (or until crumbs are golden).

4. To make seafood sauce, combine all ingredients thoroughly. Serve with kebabs.

Serves 4–6

Oyster Spring Rolls

INGREDIENTS

oil

Dipping Sauce
1 green onion, sliced diagonally
2 tablespoons/25mL rice wine vinegar
2 tablespoons/25mL reduced-salt soy sauce
1 tablespoon/15mL lime or lemon juice

2 tablespoons/25mL grated fresh ginger
    or pickled ginger
1 tablespoon/15mL chopped cilantro or dill
1 tablespoon/15mL finely chopped chives or
    green onion
1 teaspoon/5mL lime or lemon juice
5 sheets spring roll pastry
    wrappers or 20 wonton wraps
20 fresh oysters, shucked
    or 1 jar (about 20 oysters) drained

METHOD

1. Preheat oven to 350°F/180°C. Lightly spray or brush a baking tray with unsaturated oil.

2. To make dipping sauce, place green onion, vinegar, soy sauce and lime juice in a small serving bowl. Mix to combine and set aside.

3. Place ginger, cilantro or dill, chives or green onion and lime or lemon juice in a small bowl. Mix to combine.

4. Cut each sheet of spring roll pastry into four squares. Place an oyster on the centre of each square. Top with a little of the ginger mixture. Brush edges with water. Fold in sides and roll up.

5. Place rolls, seam side down, on prepared baking tray. Bake for 10–12 minutes or until pastry is crisp and golden. Serve with dipping sauce.

Makes 20 mini spring rolls

Scallops and Prawns en Brochette

INGREDIENTS

9 pickling onions

6 bacon strips

1lb/500g green prawns,
   peeled, deveined, tail intact

14oz/400g scallops

2 tablespoons/25mL olive oil

4 tablespoons/60mL melted butter

2 tablespoons/25mL fresh dill, chopped

2 tablespoons/25mL parsley, chopped

2 green onions, finely chopped

2 cloves garlic, crushed

freshly ground black pepper

2 teaspoons/10mL grated lemon rind

2 tablespoons/25mL lemon juice

METHOD

1. Parboil onions until almost tender. Drain and rinse under cold water. Cut each bacon strip into 3 and roll each section up.

2. Thread prawns, scallops and bacon onto skewers. Finish with an onion on the end of each one.

3. Combine oil, butter, dill, parsley, green onions, garlic, pepper, lemon rind and juice. Pour over seafood skewers and marinate for at least 1 hour.

4. Remove from marinade cook on preheated barbecue grill until tender, brushing occasionally with marinade.

Makes 9

Scallops Baked in Filo with Lemon Butter

INGREDIENTS

Sauce

1 tablespoon/15mL butter
2 tablespoons/25mL minced shallot
$1/2$ cup/125mL/4fl oz dry white wine
2 tablespoons/25mL whipping cream

Scallops

6 filo pastry sheets
$1/2$ cup/125mL/4fl oz melted butter
8 large sea scallops
1 tablespoon/15mL brandy
salt and pepper

1 egg yolk
2 tablespoons/25mL butter
2 tablespoons/25mL lemon juice
salt and pepper

METHOD

Sauce

1. Melt butter in small heavy saucepan over medium heat.

2. Add shallot and sauté 3 minutes.

3. Add wine and boil for 5 minutes or until liquid is reduced to $1/4$ cup/50mL.

4. Stir in cream.

Scallops

1. Place 1 filo sheet on work surface (keep remaining filo covered). Brush with butter.

2. Top with second sheet. Brush with butter.

3. Top with third sheet. Cut filo stack into four 6in/15cm squares.

4. Place one scallop in center of each square. Brush scallops with brandy. Season with salt and pepper.

5. Pull up all sides of filo around scallops to form pouches. Pinch center to seal.

6. Arrange pouches on baking sheet. Brush with melted butter.

7. Preheat oven to 425°F/220°C. Bake pouches for 10 minutes or until golden.

8. Re-heat sauce over medium-low heat. Whisk in yolk; do not boil. Add butter and whisk until just melted. Add lemon juice and season with salt and pepper. Spoon sauce onto plates and top with pastry pouches.

Serves 4

Gratin of Scallops and Mushrooms

INGREDIENTS

4 large fresh scallops

2/3 cup/150mL/5fl oz milk

2/3 cup/150mL/5fl oz heavy or whipping cream

1/4 cup/50mL all-purpose flour

2 tablespoons/25mL butter

1/4 teaspoon/1mL freshly grated nutmeg

1/2 cup/125mL diced Gruyère or Lancashire cheese

1 1/2 cups/375mL button mushroooms, trimmed and halved

2 tablespoons/25mL butter

METHOD

1. Trim the scallops, remove the orange coral and cut the white flesh of each scallop into 8 pieces.

2. Pour the milk into a non-stick saucepan. Add the scallops (except for the corals), bring to the boil and simmer for 5 minutes. Remove the scallops from the milk and set aside.

3. Add the cream, flour, butter and nutmeg and whisk gently over a low heat until the sauce thickens. Add the cheese and allow to melt without letting it boil.

4. Sauté mushrooms in butter for 2–3 minutes.

5. Spoon some scallops onto the center of each serving plate. Arrange mushrooms around the scallops. Drizzle any juices over the mushrooms.

6. Top scallop pieces with corals and pour heated sauce over top.

Serves 4

Skewered Scallops in Orange Butter

INGREDIENTS

1lb/500g fresh scallops
metal skewers

Orange Butter
1/2 cup/125mL butter
1 teaspoon/5mL brown sugar
2 teaspoons/10mL orange zest
1/3 cup/75mL orange juice

METHOD

1. Remove any brown membrane from the scallops and rinse well. Leave the coral attached. Pat dry with paper towel and thread onto metal skewers.

2. Melt the butter in a saucepan and stir in the remaining ingredients. Brush over the skewered scallops.

3. Cook under a hot grill for 2 minutes each side, brushing with the orange butter as they cook.

4. Place on serving plate and pour over the remaining hot melted butter. Serve immediately.

Serves 4

Note: The skewered scallops may also be cooked on the barbecue or grill. Cook for 1 minute each side over direct heat.

SCALLOPS & OYSTERS IN THEIR SHELLS

Grilled Oysters with Champagne and Cream

INGREDIENTS

12 fresh oysters in their shells

**3 tablespoons/45mL champagne,
dry sparkling wine or dry vermouth**

2 tablespoons/25mL butter

**2 tablespoons/25mL heavy or
whipping cream**

black pepper

1½ cups/375mL baby spinach

METHOD

1. To open oysters, see page 5. Scoop out each oyster with a teaspoon and strain the juices into a small saucepan. Remove and discard the muscle from the 12 rounded half shells, then wash and dry the shells. Place in a flameproof dish lined with crumpled foil so that the shells sit level.

2. Bring the oyster juices to a simmer and poach the oysters for 30–60 seconds, until just firm. Remove from the pan. Add the champagne to the pan and boil for 2 minutes to reduce. Remove from the heat and whisk in the butter, then the cream. Season with pepper.

3. Preheat the grill to high. Cook the spinach in a saucepan for 2–3 minutes, until wilted. Squeeze out the excess liquid and divide between the shells. Top with an oyster and spoon over a little sauce. Cook close to the grill for 1 minute or until heated through.

Serves 4

Poached Scallops with Ginger and Green Onion

INGREDIENTS

1lb/500g fresh scallops

4 green onions

1 medium carrot

4 sprigs flatleaf parsley

3/4 cup/175mL water

1/4 cup/50mL lemon juice

1 teaspoon/5mL soy sauce

2 teaspoons/10mL honey

2 teaspoons/10mL grated fresh ginger

METHOD

1. Remove any dark membrane from the scallops leaving coral attached. Rinse well.

2. Wash and peel green onions and carrot, cut into julienne strips. Pluck the parsley leaves from the stalks and rinse.

3. Heat water, lemon juice, soy sauce, honey and ginger to simmering point. Add the scallops, julienne strips and parsley and poach for 3–4 minutes. Do not overcook.

4. Remove to individual scallop shells or entrée dishes with a slotted spoon. Strain the poaching liquid, return to the saucepan and reduce over quick heat to intensify the flavor. Spoon over the scallops and serve immediately.

Serves 4

Oysters Rockefeller

INGREDIENTS

rock salt

12 medium oysters in shell

2 tablespoons/25mL onion,
    finely chopped

2 tablespoons/25mL parsley, chopped

2 tablespoons/25mL celery,
    finely chopped

1/4 cup/50mL butter (or margarine)

1/2 cup/125mL chopped fresh spinach

1/3 cup/75mL dry breadcrumbs

1/4 teaspoon/1mL salt

7 drops red pepper sauce

dash ground anise

METHOD

1. Fill two 9in/23cm glass pie dishes with rock salt to 1/2 in/1cm deep; sprinkle with water. Scrub oysters in shell under running cold water. Break off thin end of shell with hammer. Force a table knife or shucking knife between shell at broken point; pull apart. Cut oyster at muscle to separate from shell.

2. Remove any bits of shell and place oyster on deep half of shell. Arrange filled shells on rock salt bases. Heat oven to 450°F/230°C. In a saucepan cook onion, parsley and celery in butter, stirring constantly, until onion is tender.

3. Mix in remaining ingredients. Spoon about 1 tablespoon/15mL spinach mixture onto each oyster. Bake 10 minutes.

Makes 12 oysters

Oysters Acapulco

INGREDIENTS

Cilantro Pesto

1/2 cup/125mL cilantro leaves

2 tablespoons/25mL pine nuts, toasted

1 clove garlic, roughly chopped

2 tablespoons/25mL Parmesan cheese,
  grated

2 tablespoons/25mL pecorino cheese,
  grated

1/4 cup/50mL/1 1/2fl oz olive oil

salt and freshly ground black pepper

Oysters

24 oysters (or clams or mussels)
  on the half shell

rock salt (optional)

1/4 cup/50mL cilantro pesto

1/2 cup/125mL finely diced red
  bell pepper

1/2 cup/125mL crumbled Cacique
  or feta cheese

METHOD

Cilantro Pesto

1. Place the cilantro, pine nuts, garlic and cheeses in a food processor, and process, until a paste.With the motor still running, add oil in a steady stream, until well combined.

2. Season with salt and pepper, to taste. Store in fridge, with a little olive oil over top, to prevent cilantro going brown.

1. Heat grill. If grilling oysters, make a bed of rock salt in 2 baking pans and arrange the oysters in them. (If barbecueing, the oysters will go directly on the grill.)

2. Top each oyster with cilantro pesto, diced red bell pepper and crumbled Cacique or feta cheese. Cook under grill until cheese has lightly browned

Makes 24 oysters

Oysters Greta Garbo

INGREDIENTS

3 dozen oysters in shells

juice of 1/2 lime or lemon

6 slices smoked salmon
   (cut into fine strips)

1 cup/250mL/8fl oz sour cream

2 tablespoons/25mL fresh chives,
   chopped, for garnish

red caviar for garnish

crushed ice for serving

METHOD

1. Sprinkle the oysters with lime or lemon juice and top with smoked salmon.

2. Put a dollop of the sour cream onto each oyster.

3. Garnish with chives and red caviar. Serve on a bed of ice.

Serves 6 (as an entrée)

Oysters and Mussels in Shells

INGREDIENTS

1lb/500g mussels, scrubbed and
   beards removed

24 oysters in half shells

4 tablespoons/60mL butter, softened

1 tablespoon/15mL fresh parsley,
   chopped

2 tablespoons/25mL lemon juice

1 tablespoon/15mL orange juice

1 tablespoon/15mL white wine

METHOD

1. Preheat barbecue to a high heat. Place mussels and oysters on barbecue grill and cook for 3–5 minutes or until mussel shells open and oysters are warm. Discard any mussels that do not open after 5 minutes of cooking.

2. Place butter, parsley, lemon juice, orange juice and wine in a heavy-based saucepan. Place on barbecue and cook, stirring, for 2 minutes or until mixture is bubbling.

3. Place mussels and oysters on a serving platter, drizzle with butter mixture and serve immediately.

Serves 6

Note: Mussels will live out of water for up to 7 days if treated correctly. To keep mussels alive, place them in a bucket, cover with a wet towel and top with ice. Store in a cool place and as the ice melts, drain off the water and replace ice. It is important that the mussels do not sit in the water or they will drown.

OYSTERS GRETA GARBO

Chardonnay Oysters

INGREDIENTS

36 freshly opened oysters
crushed ice

Chardonnay Vinaigrette
3 green onions, finely sliced
¹/₃ cup/75mL/3fl oz dry chardonnay wine
2 tablespoons/25mL cider vinegar
1 tablespoon/15mL light vegetable oil
crushed black peppercorns to taste

METHOD

1. Arrange oysters on a serving platter lined with crushed ice.

2. To make vinaigrette, place green onions, wine, vinegar, oil and black peppercorns in a bowl and whisk to combine. Just prior to serving, spoon a little vinaigrette over each oyster.

Serves 6

Oysters Kilpatrick

INGREDIENTS

24 oysters on the shell
1 teaspoon/5mL Worcestershire sauce
1 cup/250mL/8fl oz cream
pepper and salt
8oz/250g bacon strips, finely chopped
fine breadcrumbs

METHOD

1. Remove oysters from shells and put aside. Put shells on a baking sheet and heat in a moderate oven. Mix Worcestershire sauce and cream. When shells are hot, return oysters to shells. Use tongs to handle the shells, as they get very hot. Add a little of the cream mixture to each shell and sprinkle with pepper and salt.

2. Top each oyster with chopped bacon and fine breadcrumbs. Place baking sheet under a hot grill and grill until bacon is crisp but not burnt and oysters are warmed through.

Note: Oysters Kilpatrick are very tasty served with a bowl of hot puréed spinach and thin slices of buttered brown or rye bread.

Serves 2–4 as an entrée

Scallops with Mango Salsa

INGREDIENTS

Mango Salsa

1 mango, peeled and chopped

1 tablespoon/15mL fresh mint, chopped

1 tablespoon/15mL lemon juice

2 tablespoons/25mL sesame seeds, toasted

16 scallops in half shells

freshly ground black pepper

METHOD

1. To make salsa, place mango, mint, lemon juice and sesame seeds in a small bowl and mix to combine. Cover and refrigerate until required.

2. Bring a large saucepan of water to the boil. Add scallops and cook for 1 minute or until tender. Using a slotted spoon, remove scallops from water and place on individual half shells on a serving platter. Serve warm or chilled, seasoned with black pepper and topped with salsa.

Makes 16

Oysters with Smoked Salmon

INGREDIENTS

**8oz/250g smoked salmon slices or
  gravlax**
16 oysters in the shell
3 tablespoons/45mL lemon juice
freshly ground black pepper

METHOD

1. Cut smoked salmon or gravlax into long
strips. Loosen oysters in shells.

2. Top oysters with smoked salmon or gravlax
slices. Sprinkle with lemon juice and season
with black pepper. Cover and refrigerate until
required.

Makes 16

Scallops Baked with Cured Ham

INGREDIENTS

2 tablespoons/25mL olive oil

1lb/500g scallops, in half shell

salt and freshly ground black pepper

1/2 cup/125mL minced onion

1 garlic clove, minced

1/4 cup/50mL minced cured ham, such as prosciutto

3 tablespoons/45mL dry white wine

1/2 cup/125mL breadcrumbs

1 tablespoon/15mL minced parsely

1 teaspoon/5mL lemon juice

METHOD

1. Heat 1 tablespoon/15mL of the oil in a large skillet and sauté the scallops over high heat for 1 minute. Divide the scallops among the shells and sprinkle with salt and pepper.

2. Add the onion and garlic and a little more oil, if necessary, to the skillet. Cover and cook over low heat for 15 minutes. Add the ham and sauté 1 minute. Stir in the wine and let it cook off. Spoon mixture over scallops. Pre-heat the oven to 450°F/230°C.

3. In a small bowl, combine the bread crumbs, parsley, lemon juice and remaining oil. Sprinkle over the scallops. Place shells on baking sheet and bake 10 minutes. If necessary, run under the grill to brown the top crumbs.

Serves 2 (or 4 as tapas)

Hot Oysters and Leeks

INGREDIENTS

20–24 large oysters in the half shell
coarse sea salt
1 small leek, washed and finely sliced
2 tablespoons/25mL butter
salt, pepper and a pinch of sugar
squeeze of lemon juice
$^{1}/_{2}$ cup/125mL dry white wine
pinch of saffron threads
   or curry powder
$^{1}/_{2}$ cup/125mL cream
1 egg yolk
salt and white pepper

METHOD

1. Remove the oysters from their shells and keep chilled. Wash the shells and arrange in 4 individual gratin dishes, on a bed of coarse sea salt to keep them level.

2. Wash leek and slice it finely. Melt butter in a pan and toss the leek in the hot butter. Season with salt, freshly ground pepper and sugar, cover tightly and cook gently until tender. Season with lemon juice.

3. Boil the wine with the saffron or curry powder over a moderate heat until reduced by half. In a small bowl combine the cream with the egg yolk and whisk. Whisk in the hot wine mixture and return to gentle heat to thicken slightly, whisking all the time. Do not let it boil. Add salt and white pepper to taste and remove from heat.

4. Arrange the cooked leeks in the oyster shells and place oysters on top. Coat each oyster with the sauce and place under a preheated hot grill for a minute or so to glaze. Serve immediately.

Serves 4

Steamed Scallops with Black Beans and Garlic

INGREDIENTS

12 large scallops (or 24 small scallops)
1 tablespoon/15mL dry sherry
1 tablespoon/15mL Chinese salted black beans
1 teaspoon/5mL freshly crushed garlic
3 teaspoons/15mL soy sauce
1/4 teaspoon/1mL salt
pinch cracked black peppercorns
1/2 teaspoon/2mL sugar
1 teaspoon/5mL oil
1 teaspoon/5mL cornstarch
1 tablespoon/15mL Asian sesame oil
1 green onion (green part only), cut into fine slices
12 cilantro leaves
1/2 hot chili, seeded and cut into 5mm/1/4 in diamond shapes

METHOD

1. Use the 12 scallop shells for the cooking and serving dishes. Mix scallops with the sherry, and then place one scallop in each shell. Set aside.

2. Soak the black beans covered in cold water for 15 minutes, then rinse, dry on paper towels, and mince. Combine beans, garlic, soy sauce, salt, pepper, sugar, oil and cornstarch. Distribute some of this mixture over each of the scallops, and trickle the sesame oil over each scallop.

3. Bring a few inches of water to a vigorous boil in a steamer. Place the scallops on a steamer rack, cover tightly, and steam for 5 minutes. Remove, sprinkle with green onions, and garnish each scallop with one cilantro leaf and a hot chili diamond before serving.

Serves 4

Oysters Bloody Mary

INGREDIENTS

6 scrubbed oysters, opened

splash of vodka

dash of Tabasco sauce

grind of black pepper

squeeze of fresh lime

flesh of 2 fresh tomatoes,
    chopped (no pulp or seeds)

$1/2$–1 teaspoon/2–5mL whole grain
    mustard (optional)

lime and pepper for serving

METHOD

1. Combine the ingredients and spread evenly over the opened oysters. Chill or grill for 5–10 minutes. Serve with bread and butter, or hot buttered toast. Ensure extra lime and pepper are available.

Makes 6 oysters

SEAFOOD SOUPS

Creamy Scallop Soup with Mushroom-Asparagus Duxelles

INGREDIENTS

2 tablespoons/25mL butter

2 shallots, minced

3 cups/750mL mushrooms, minced
  (reserve one), cut into 8 thin slices

8 spears asparagus (reserve tips), minced

2 tablespoons/25mL all-purpose flour

4 cups/1L milk

concentrated fish (or scallop) stock,
  which would dilute to 4 cups/1L

8oz/250g sea scallops, cut into
  bite-sized pieces

1/2 cup/125mL heavy or whipping cream

1/4 cup/50mL dry white wine

pinches of paprika to garnish

METHOD

1. In a saucepan, melt butter, add minced shallots, minced mushrooms, and minced asparagus, and saute on low heat for 10 minutes, stirring occasionally. When flavors are concentrated, stir in the flour and cook for a minute or two, then slowly whisk in the milk. When the soup begins to thicken, whisk in the fish or seafood stock and let simmer for a minute or two.

2. Add the scallops, reserved asparagus tips, and reserved mushroom slices and simmer for 3 minutes. Pour in the cream, reheat, and simmer for a few more minutes.

3. When ready to serve, pour in the wine, then ladle the soup into soup bowls, evenly dividing the scallops, mushroom slices, and asparagus tips. Garnish with a pinch of fresh paprika and serve immediately.

Serves 4

Creamy Oyster Bisque

INGREDIENTS

20 fresh oysters, shucked, or 1 jar drained,
   liquid reserved

low-salt fish or vegetable stock

1/2 cup/125mL white wine

1 small white onion or 1/2 leek, diced

1 stalk celery, diced

2 cups/500mL diced peeled potato

1 tablespoon/15mL chopped fresh thyme or
   1 teaspoon/5mL dried thyme

1/2 cup/125mL low-fat milk

freshly ground black pepper

sprigs watercress or fresh parsley, optional

METHOD

1. Measure liquid from oysters. Add stock to make up to 1 cup/250mL/8fl oz.

2. Heat 2 tablespoons/25mL of the wine in a large saucepan over a low heat. Add onion and celery. Cook, stirring, for 4–5 minutes or until onion is transparent. Add potato and thyme. Stir in stock mixture and remaining wine. Bring to boil and simmer for 10–15 minutes or until potatoes are soft and most of the liquid is absorbed. Cool slightly.

3. Transfer mixture to a food processor or blender. Add half the oysters, the milk and black pepper to taste. Purée. Return mixture to a clean saucepan. Bring to the boil. Remove soup from heat and stir in remaining oysters.

4. To serve, ladle soup into warm bowls and top with watercress or parsley sprigs, if desired.

Serves 4

Irish Oyster Soup

INGREDIENTS

2 large potatoes, unpeeled

4 cups/1L milk

bouquet garni (a bay leaf and green
herbs tied together or in a tea ball)

3 tablespoons/45mL butter

4oz/125g salt pork, diced

salt and pepper

36 fresh shucked oysters, juice reserved

chopped parsley to garnish

METHOD

1. Cook the potatoes in boiling salted water until just tender. Meanwhile, bring the milk to a boil, remove from heat, dunk in the bouquet garni, and allow to infuse. Then sauté the diced salt pork in a little of the butter over low heat until it is just cooked through.

2. When the potatoes are done, peel and mash, then whip in the hot herbed milk. Add the salt pork drained of its grease. Season to taste. Bring to a boil, stirring constantly, then add the oysters with their liquid. Simmer for a few minutes. Taste for seasoning and stir in the rest of the butter.

Serves 6–8

Note: You can make a nice presentation from a tureen at the table or just ladle into bowls in the kitchen and serve at once, garnished with chopped parsley.

Manhattan Oyster Chowder

INGREDIENTS

2 tablespoons/25mL olive oil

1 onion, chopped into bite-sized chunks

1$^1/_2$ cups/375mL dark-gilled mushrooms, quartered

2 cloves garlic, chopped

3 cups/750mL fish stock

14oz/398mL can of tomatoes, seeded and chopped

bay leaf

$^1/_4$ teaspoon/1mL rosemary, crushed to a powder

$^1/_4$ teaspoon/1mL oregano, crushed to a powder

pinch hot pepper flakes

1 zucchini, cut into bite-sized chunks

1 jar standard oysters

parsley

METHOD

1. Heat oil in large saucepan and sauté the onions and mushrooms until the onions are golden and the mushrooms are brown. Add garlic and stir for a minute. Add fish stock and chopped tomatoes with their juice. Stir in the bay leaf, rosemary, oregano and hot pepper flakes. Bring to a boil, then reduce heat and simmer, partially covered, for 25 minutes.

2. Add zucchini, cover and simmer another 10 minutes, until the zucchini is almost tender. Slip the oysters with their liquid into the soup and cook, uncovered, just until the edges of the oysters begin to curl. (You want them tender, not chewy.)

3. Ladle into bowls. Sprinkle with parsley and serve immediately. Fat, dense oyster biscuits taste very good with this soup.

Serves 4

Note: This spicy and chunky chowder is just the thing for a warming lunch or a light dinner with lots of side dishes.

Oyster and Brie Soup

INGREDIENTS

3 dozen small to medium
   oysters in their liquor
4 cups/1L cold water
1/2 cup/125mL unsalted butter
1/4 –1/2 cup/50–125mL all-purpose flour
1 cup/250mL onion, coarsely chopped
1/2 stalk celery, coarsely chopped
1/2 teaspoon/2mL white pepper
1/2 teaspoon/2mL ground red pepper
1lb/500g brie cheese, cut in small pieces
2 cups/500mL heavy or whipping cream
1/2 bunch green onions, chopped
1/2 cup/125mL champagne (optional)
1 handful cured smoked ham,
   finely chopped
8oz/250g bacon, fried and crumbled

METHOD

1. Combine oysters and water and refrigerate for 1 hour.

2. Strain the oysters and reserve the water.

3. In a large skillet, melt the butter over low heat. Add the flour and whisk until smooth. Add the onion and celery and sauté about 3 minutes, stirring occasionally. Stir in the pepper and sauté 2 minutes and set aside.

4. In a large saucepan, bring the oyster water to a boil. Stir in vegetable mixture. Turn heat to high. Add cheese; cook for 2 minutes, stirring constantly, until cheese starts to melt. Lower heat to a simmer and continue cooking for about 4 minutes, stirring constantly.

5. Remove from heat, strain soup and return to pot. Turn heat to high and cook 1 minute, stirring constantly. Stir in cream, cook until close to a boil (about 2 minutes). Add green onions and champagne if desired.

6. Lower heat and add the oysters and handful of cured smoked ham. Check the seasoning at this point and add red pepper and salt to taste. When oysters curl, serve immediately in bread bowls with crumbled bacon to garnish the top.

Serves 4

Oyster Cream Soup with Lemony Carrots

INGREDIENTS

2 whole carrots, peeled

2 tablespoons/25mL lemon juice

1 tablespoon/15mL olive oil

2 tablespoons/25mL butter

2 medium onions, chopped

1 bunch green onions, chopped

3 garlic cloves, chopped

4 canned tomatoes (or 2 fresh),
**   peeled, seeded, and chopped**

1 teaspoon/5mL basil, chopped
**   (or pesto)**

1 teaspoon/5mL thyme

salt and white pepper

cayenne pepper

5 cups/1.25L milk

1 cup/250mL/8fl oz whipping cream

20oz/570g jar of oysters

basil leaves or pesto for garnish

METHOD

1. Boil the carrots until tender. Drain, slice thinly and mix with lemon juice and oil. Refrigerate.

2. Melt the butter in a large saucepan over medium-low heat. Add onions, green onions and garlic and cook until translucent (about 10 minutes). Add the tomatoes, increase heat and cook for 10 minutes or until thickened, stirring occasionally. Stir in the basil and thyme, salt, pepper and cayenne to taste. Cook until all the moisture has evaporated, then purée in a blender or food processor. At this point, you can refrigerate until ready to serve.

3. When ready to eat, stir the onion mixture into a saucepan with the milk and cream and bring to a boil. Reduce heat, season, and add the carrots with marinade. Add the whole jar of oysters, including the liquid, and poach for 2 minutes or until just opaque.

4. Ladle into flat soup bowls and garnish with the basil leaves or swirl a teaspoon of pesto through each bowl.

Serves 6

Note: A thick, tangy soup to serve as a warming lunch or light supper with lots of bread and salad.

Hot and Sour Scallop Soup

INGREDIENTS

4 cups/1L canned low-sodium
  chicken broth

1 cup/250mL mushrooms, thinly sliced

1/4 cup/50mL bamboo shoots, sliced

1/2lb/250g sea or bay scallops, sliced
  1/4in/5mm thick

1 teaspoon/5mL low-sodium soy sauce

1/4 teaspoon/1mL white pepper

2 tablespoons/25mL cornstarch

3 tablespoons/45mL warm water

1 egg, beaten

3 tablespoons/45mL rice vinegar
  (2 tablespoons/25mL white wine vinegar
  may be substituted)

1/3 cup/75mL thinly sliced green onions

METHOD

1. Place chicken broth, mushrooms and bamboo shoots in saucepan. Bring to the boil, reduce heat and simmer 5 minutes. Rinse scallops under cold running water. Add scallops, soy sauce and pepper.

2. Bring to the boil. Mix the cornstarch with warm water. Add cornstarch mixture and stir a few seconds until thickened. Stir briskly with a chopstick and gradually pour in egg. Remove from heat. Stir in vinegar and sprinkle with green onion. Serve immediately.

Serves 4

Oyster Hots

INGREDIENTS

6 cups/1.5L fish stock

2 potatoes, cut into a fine julienne

2 carrots, cut into a fine julienne

1/2 red bell pepper, cut into a
fine julienne

1/2 to 1 jalapeno pepper, cut into
fine slivers

1/2 teaspoon/2 mL grated lemon zest

1/4 teaspoon/1mL thyme

salt and white pepper

1 jar standard oysters

juice of 1 lemon
(2–3 tablespoons/25–45mL)

paper thin rounds of lemon, sprinkled
with thyme to garnish

METHOD

1. Bring the stock to a the boil in a large saucepan. Add potatoes, carrots, red bell pepper, jalapeno slivers, lemon zest, thyme and salt and pepper to taste. Reduce heat, leave uncovered and simmer for 15 minutes or until the vegetables are tender.

2. Slip the oysters with their liquid into the simmering stock and cook for 2 minutes just until their edges curl. Remove from heat, stir in lemon juice, and adjust for seasoning. Ladle into bowls, top each with a lemon slice and sprinkling of thyme. Serve immediately.

Serves 4–6

Note: So clean and piquant, you'll think you've been to the beach; serve hot as a stimulating first course.

Turmeric-Infused Scallop Soup

INGREDIENTS

2 tablespoons/25mL unsalted butter

1/2 teaspoon/2mL turmeric

1 1/2 lb/750g scallops

3 shallots, finely chopped

1 bottle dry white wine

4 cups/1L fish stock

1/2 cup/125mL crème fraîche
  (see page 12)

3 1/2 cups/875mL heavy or
  whipping cream

freshly ground white pepper

1/2 teaspoon/2mL white wine vinegar

salt to taste

METHOD

1. In a large saucepan cook butter, turmeric, scallops and shallots over moderately low heat, stirring until shallots are softened. Add wine and stock and simmer mixture until reduced by half. Take off heat and allow to cool.

2. Pour soup into a blender, and blend until smooth. Put back onto heat in a saucepan, add crème fraîche and 3 cups/750mL of the heavy or whipping cream and simmer, stirring occasionally, for 15 minutes.

3. Pour soup through a fine sieve into a heatproof bowl. Stir in white pepper, vinegar and salt to taste. In another bowl whisk remaining 1/2 cup/125mL heavy cream until thickened and stir into soup until incorporated. Serve with wedge of herbed flatbread.

Serves 10

Rich Scallop Soup

INGREDIENTS

2 cups/500mL/16fl oz milk

1 cup/250mL/8fl oz heavy or
   whipping cream

2 tablespoons/25mL butter
   or margarine

1 teaspoon/5mL salt

$1/4$ teaspoon/1mL white pepper

1 teaspoon/5mL Worcestershire
   sauce

1lb/500g scallops, chopped into
   small pieces

paprika

3 tablespoons/45mL parsley, fresh,
   finely chopped

METHOD

1. In the top of a double boiler, blend milk, cream, butter or margarine, salt, pepper and Worcestershire sauce. Fill the bottom with boiling water and bring to a simmer, stirring frequently. Add scallops to the mixture and cook until tender about 8–10 minutes. Pour hot soup into individual bowls. Sprinkle each bowl with paprika and parsley.

Serves 6

SCALLOP &
OYSTER SALADS

Barbecued Seafood Salad

INGREDIENTS

2 tablespoons/25mL lemon juice

1 tablespoon/15mL olive oil

10^1/$_2$oz/300g firm white fish (such as swordfish, mackerel or cod), cut into 1in/2.5cm cubes

10^1/$_2$oz/300g pink fish (such as salmon, marlin or tuna)

12 scallops

12 uncooked prawns (with or without shell)

1 calamari (squid), cleaned and tube cut into rings, (discard the tentacles or freeze for another use)

Raspberry and Tarragon Dressing

3 tablespoons/45mL fresh tarragon, chopped

2 tablespoons/25mL raspberry or red wine vinegar

2 tablespoons/25mL lemon juice

1 tablespoon/15mL olive oil

freshly ground black pepper

1 bunch watercress, broken into sprigs

1 large red onion, cut into rings

1 long English cucumber, sliced thinly

METHOD

1. Place lemon juice and oil in a bowl. Whisk to combine. Add white and pink fish, scallops, prawns and calamari. Toss to combine. Cover and marinate in the refrigerator for 1 hour or until ready to use (do not marinate for longer than 2 hours).

2. For the dressing, place tarragon, vinegar, lemon juice, oil and black pepper to taste in a screwtop jar. Shake to combine and set aside.

3. Preheat a barbecue or grill until very hot. Line a serving platter with watercress.

4. Drain seafood mixture. Place on barbecue plate or in pan. Add onion and cook, turning several times, for 6–8 minutes or until seafood is just cooked. Take care not to overcook or the seafood will be tough and dry.

5. Transfer seafood mixture to a bowl. Add cucumber and dressing. Toss to combine. Spoon seafood mixture over watercress. Serve immediately.

Serves 8

Oyster Salad

INGREDIENTS

24 oysters, on the half shell or meat only

1 head lettuce

6 teaspoons/30mL lemon juice

2 tomatoes, sliced thinly

1 cup/250mL celery, diced

mayonnaise

paprika

METHOD

1. Cook oysters in their own juice until the edges curl up. Drain and chill.

2. Place a lettuce leaf on 4 salad plates. Shred rest of lettuce and place on lettuce leaves.

3. Lay 6 oysters on each lettuce leaf and sprinkle with lemon juice.

4. Place tomato and celery on top. Dab oysters with mayonnaise, sprinkle with paprika, and chill for 1 hour before serving.

Serves 4

Note: If your oysters have no shells, just place in a baking dish to cook.

Spinach Salad with Scallops

INGREDIENTS

1lb/500g fresh scallops

1/2 cup/125mL orange juice

1/2 cup/125mL dry white wine

1/2 teaspoon/2mL salt

4 cups/1L baby spinach leaves, washed and crisped

2 medium-sized oranges, segmented

Dressing

1/4 cup/50mL orange juice

2 teaspoons/10mL finely chopped parsley

1/3 cup/75mL olive oil

1 teaspoon/5mL balsamic vinegar

1/2 teaspoon/2mL sugar

pinch salt

METHOD

1. Remove any brown membrane from the scallops, rinse well. Detach the coral and separate

2. Heat orange juice, wine and salt to simmering point, add white scallops and poach for 2 minutes. Add the coral and poach 1 minute more. Do not overcook. Remove to a bowl with the juice and refrigerate to cool. Drain the scallops before inclusion in the salad.

3. Toss the spinach, orange segments and drained scallops quickly together. Combine dressing ingredients in a screwtop jar, shake well, and toss through the salad. Serve in individual entrée dishes.

Serves 4

Tips: To segment the orange, peel the orange taking off all of the pith. With a small sharp knife cut between the membrane lines to remove each segment.

To crisp the spinach, place the washed spinach in a clean towel and refrigerate for 1 hour.

Scallop and Bacon Salad

INGREDIENTS

a few handfuls endive

1 cucumber, diced

cherry tomatoes, quartered

olive oil

juice of 1 lemon or lime

vinegar

salt and pepper

3 strips streaky bacon

8 scallops, shells removed

METHOD

1. Mix the salad of endive, cucumber, and tomatoes in a large bowl, and dress with a little oil, half the lemon or lime juice and vinegar and season with salt and pepper.

2. Fry the bacon in a little olive oil on a low heat, until crispy. Remove and set aside on paper towels.

3. Fry the scallops in the bacon fat for only a few minutes on each side. They should adopt a lovely golden color. Season lightly, and squeeze in the remaining lemon juice. Remove from heat.

4. Put some salad on a plate and place a few scallops on top. Break up the bacon and scatter the pieces over. Pour over some of the juices from the pan and serve.

Serves 2

Note: For a bit of a twist you could serve small portions of this in the scallop shells.

Salad of Scallops on Bitter Greens with Strawberries

INGREDIENTS

1lb/500g scallops

3 tablespoons/45mL olive oil

salad greens – enough iceberg, arugula, mizuna,
    chicory or yellow section of curly endive leaves
    to make a mound and cover the base of
    6 entrée plates (use any leafy mixture
    you fancy)

Vinaigrette

3/4 cup/175mL olive oil

3 tablespoons/45mL raspberry vinegar

salt and pepper

2 tablespoons/25mL chopped chives, finely cut

olive oil for stir-frying scallops

about 20 small strawberries, washed and halved

1 Granny Smith apple, unpeeled, in very small
    cubes or slices (squeeze a lemon over to
    prevent browning)

METHOD

1. Place scallops in a bowl with the oil and marinate for
1 hour. Divide salad greens amongst the plates.

2. Shake vinaigrette ingredients together in a jar.

3. Add olive oil to a heavy-based wok or fry pan and
on medium to high heat, quickly stir-fry scallops for
30 seconds or until seared very light brown, about
30 seconds but don't crowd them or they will stew.

4. Spoon scallops over salad greens, scatter
strawberries and apple cubes all over, shake
vinaigrette and drizzle over the top.

5. Sprinkle with chives and serve immediately.

Serves 4–6

Note: Other berries, such as raspberries,
can be used when in season.

Scallop and Watercress Salad

INGREDIENTS

Dressing

2/3 cup/150mL/5fl oz walnut oil
    or olive oil
2 tablespoons/25mL red wine vinegar
2 small cloves garlic, minced
salt
white pepper

10 fresh scallops
3 cups/750mL watercress, discard woody
    stems, select tender tips only
1 cup/250mL water chestnuts, halved
1/2 cup/125mL cherry tomatoes
1/2 cup/125mL walnut halves
1 cup/250mL bean sprouts, topped
    and tailed

METHOD

1. Mix the dressing ingredients together in a jar and shake well.

2. Place the scallops on a plate suitable for steaming. Sprinkle the scallops with a little of the dressing and steam gently over boiling water for 6 minutes.

3. Wash and dry the watercress, and snap into 5in/12cm sections. In a serving bowl, combine the watercress, water chestnuts, cherry tomatoes, walnuts and bean sprouts. Pour on the dressing and toss through the salad. Gently mix in the scallops.

Serves 4

Grilled Sea Scallop
and Pink Grapefruit Salad

INGREDIENTS

1–1$^1/_2$ lb/500–750g sea scallops

$^1/_3$ cup/75mL grapefruit juice

1 cup/250ml/9fl oz non-fat plain yogurt

1 tablespoon/15mL honey

$^1/_3$ cup/75mL couscous, cooked
   and fluffed

1 bag mixed baby lettuce leaves

2 large pink grapefruits, peeled and
   segmented

1 large tomato, cored and diced

1 cup/250mL baby green beans, cleaned
   and cooked

$^1/_4$ package radish sprouts

fresh cracked black pepper to taste

METHOD

1. Season and grill scallops. Set aside and allow to cool. In a mixing bowl, combine grapefruit juice, yogurt, and honey.

2. Spoon couscous into base of salad bowl. Arrange mixed baby lettuce leaves in the center, top with sea scallops, pink grapefruit segments, tomato, green beans and radish sprouts. Season with fresh black cracked pepper.

Serves 4

SAUTÉED SCALLOPS WITH FETA

Sautéed Scallops with Feta

INGREDIENTS

1/2 large onion

1 1/2 red bell peppers

2 jalapeno peppers, sliced

1lb/500g large sea scallops

4 tablespoons/60mL butter

1/2 cup/125mL white wine

1/2 cup/125mL grated mozzarella cheese

1/2 cup/125mL feta cheese

pinch garlic to taste

salt to taste

chili powder to taste

METHOD

1. Sauté onion, red bell peppers, jalapenos and sea scallops in butter until soft.

2. Add white wine, cover and cook for 45 seconds. Sprinkle with mozzarella and feta. Add pinches of garlic, salt and chili powder and let simmer until cheeses melt. Serve over rice.

Serves 2

Scallop, Mussel and Asparagus Salad

INGREDIENTS

8oz/250g fresh or frozen sea scallops

6 large or 12 small fresh mussels in shells

1 cup/250mL/8fl oz water

8–10 fresh asparagus spears

oil for cooking scallops

1/3 cup/75mL/2 1/2 fl oz light sour cream

1/2 teaspoon/2mL finely shredded lime peel

2 teaspoons/10mL lime juice

2 teaspoons/10mL salmon roe or red caviar

1/8 teaspoon/1mL pepper

1 head butter lettuce

fresh chives

lime wedges

METHOD

1. Thaw scallops, if frozen. Scrub mussels under cold running water; remove beards and discard. Soak the mussels in cold salted water for 15 minutes, then drain and rinse. Repeat soaking, draining, and rinsing twice more. Set aside.

2. In a large saucepan bring the 1 cup/250mL water just to boiling. Place asparagus in saucepan and cook, covered, about 3 minutes or until crisp-tender. Do not overcook. Remove asparagus, reserving water in saucepan. Rinse asparagus in cold water then cover and chill in the refrigerator. Meanwhile, return water to just boiling. Add mussels to water and simmer, covered, for 5 minutes or until shells open. (Discard any mussels that do not open.) Drain and rinse mussels then cover and chill in the refrigerator for at least 2 hours.

3. Heat oil in non-stick skillet. Cook scallops in hot oil for 1–3 minutes or until scallops are opaque. Remove scallops and cover and chill in the refrigerator for at least 2 hours. In a small bowl, combine sour cream, lime peel, lime juice, half the roe or caviar, and the pepper. Cover and chill in the refrigerator.

4. Arrange chilled mussels, scallops, and asparagus on lettuce leaves. Serve with sour cream mixture and remaining roe or caviar. Garnish salad with chives and lime wedges.

Serves 2

Seared Scallop Salad

INGREDIENTS

Mustard Dressing

3 tablespoons/45mL mayonnaise

1 tablespoon/15mL olive oil

1 tablespoon/15mL vinegar

2 teaspoons/10mL Dijon mustard

2 teaspoons/10mL sesame oil

2 cloves garlic, crushed

12oz/375g scallops, cleaned

4 strips bacon, chopped

1 head romaine lettuce, leaves separated

1 cup/250mL croutons

fresh Parmesan cheese

METHOD

1. To make dressing, place mayonnaise, olive oil, vinegar and mustard in a bowl, mix to combine and set aside.

2. Heat sesame oil in a frying pan over a high heat, add garlic and scallops and cook, stirring, for 1 minute or until scallops just turn opaque. Remove scallop mixture from pan and set aside. Add bacon to pan and cook, stirring, for 4 minutes or until crisp. Remove bacon from pan and drain on paper towels.

3. Place lettuce leaves in a large salad bowl, add dressing and toss to coat. Add bacon, croutons and shavings of Parmesan cheese and toss to combine. Spoon scallop mixture over salad and serve.

Serves 4

Scallop Salad with Fruit Salsa

INGREDIENTS

1 small pineapple (about 3lb/1^1/3kg)

1 cup/250mL strawberries, chopped

^{3}/4 cup/175mL peach, pitted, peeled, and chopped or chopped frozen unsweetened peach slices

2 jalapeno peppers, seeded and chopped (2 tablespoons/25mL)

1–2 tablespoons/15-25mL chopped cilantro or parsley

several dashes bottled hot pepper sauce

^{1}/4 cup/50mL orange juice

12oz/375g fresh or frozen sea scallops or bay scallops

4 cups/1L boiling salted water

romaine lettuce leaves

kiwi fruit (optional) peeled, sliced

cilantro leaves (optional)

METHOD

1. Using a sharp knife cut two ^{3}/4in/2cm thick slices from the center of the pineapple. Cut each slice into six wedges. Remove the hard core from each wedge. Wrap and refrigerate the pineapple wedges. Peel, core and finely chop enough of the remaining pineapple to make ^{3}/4 cup/175mL (save the remaining pineapple for another use).

2. For salsa, combine the ^{3}/4 cup/175mL chopped pineapple, strawberries, peach, jalapeno peppers, cilantro or parsley and hot pepper sauce. Place about 1 cup/250mL of the fruit mixture into a blender or food processor with orange juice. Cover and blend or process just till pureed. Stir into remaining fruit mixture. Cover and chill for several hours or overnight, stirring occasionally.

3. Thaw scallops, if frozen. Cut large scallops in half. Bring 4 cups/1L salted water to the boil. Add scallops. Simmer, uncovered, for 1–2 minutes, stirring occasionally, or until scallops are opaque. Drain, and rinse under cold running water. Cover and chill for several hours or overnight.

4. To serve, line 4 salad plates with lettuce leaves. Arrange three of the reserved pineapple wedges on each plate, with the point of the wedge toward the center. Divide scallops among the plates. Top with salsa. If desired, garnish each plate with sliced kiwi fruit and cilantro.

Serves 4

Squid and Scallop Salad

INGREDIENTS

Herb and Balsamic Dressing

1 tablespoon/15mL fresh ginger,
   finely grated
1 tablespoon/15mL chopped
   fresh rosemary
1 clove garlic, crushed
1/4 cup/50mL olive oil
2 tablespoons/25mL lime juice
1 tablespoon/15mL balsamic or red
   wine vinegar

1 red bell pepper, seeded and halved
1 yellow or green bell pepper,
   seeded and halved
2 squid (calamari) tubes
9oz/250g scallops
8–10 asparagus spears, cut into 2in/5cm
   pieces, blanched
1 red onion, sliced
3 tablespoons/45mL cilantro leaves
1 bunch arugula or watercress

METHOD

1. To make dressing, place ginger, rosemary, garlic, oil, lime juice and vinegar in a screwtop jar and shake well to combine. Set aside.

2. Preheat barbecue to a high heat. Place red and yellow or green bell pepper halves skin side down on lightly oiled barbecue grill and cook for 5–10 minutes or until skins are blistered and charred. Place in a plastic food bag or paper bag and set aside until cool enough to handle. Remove skins and cut flesh into thin strips.

3. Cut squid (calamari) tubes lengthwise and open out flat. Using a sharp knife cut parallel lines down the length of the squid, taking care not to cut through the flesh. Make more cuts in the opposite direction to form a diamond pattern. Cut into 2in/5cm squares.

4. Place squid and scallops on lightly oiled barbecue plate (griddle) and cook, turning several times, for 3 minutes or until tender. Set aside to cool slightly.

5. Combine bell peppers, asparagus, onion and cilantro. Line a large serving platter with arugula or watercress, top with vegetables, squid and scallops. Drizzle with dressing and serve immediately.

Serves 4

Warm Seafood Salad

INGREDIENTS

6 cups/1.5L assorted salad leaves

2 or 3 yellow teardrop tomatoes (optional)

1 dozen cherry tomatoes, halved

2 avocados, pitted, peeled and sliced

1¼ cups/300mL snow peas trimmed and blanched

8–10 asparagus spears, cut into 2in/5cm pieces, blanched

Oriental Dressing

1 tablespoon/15mL rice vinegar

1 tablespoon/15mL fish sauce

2 tablespoons/25mL sweet chili sauce

1 tablespoon/15mL fresh basil, shredded

1 tablespoon/15mL lemon juice

¼ cup/50mL water

3 calamari (squid) tubes

2 tablespoons/25mL butter

9oz/250g scallops

16 uncooked medium prawns, shelled and deveined, tails left intact

7oz/200g thickly sliced smoked trout or smoked salmon

Note: This salad is great served warm, but also may be made ahead of time and served chilled. If serving chilled, prepare the salad, seafood and dressing and store separately in the refrigerator. Just prior to serving, assemble the salad as described in the recipe.

METHOD

1. Arrange salad leaves, teardrop tomatoes (if using) and cherry tomatoes, avocados, snow peas and asparagus on a large serving platter.

2. To make dressing, place vinegar, fish sauce, chili sauce, basil, lemon juice and water in a small bowl and whisk to combine.

3. Cut calamari (squid) tubes lengthwise, and open out flat. Using a sharp knife, cut parallel lines down the length of the calamari taking care not to cut right through the flesh.

Make more cuts in the opposite direction to form a diamond pattern. Cut each piece into 2in/5cm squares.

4. Melt butter in a large frying pan, add scallops and prawns and stir-fry for 3 minutes. Add calamari pieces and stir-fry for 1 minute longer. Arrange cooked seafood and smoked trout or smoked salmon on salad and drizzle with dressing.

Serves 8

MAIN MEALS

Chicken and Oyster Casserole

INGREDIENTS

2¹/₄ lb/1kg chicken thighs, skinned
   and boned
¹/₂ cup/125mL all-purpose flour
salt and black pepper
2 onions, finely chopped
4 cloves of garlic, crushed
3 cups/750mL mushrooms
1 tablespoon/15mL chopped fresh sage
³/₄ cup/175mL/6fl oz white wine
³/₄ cup/175mL/6fl oz water
zest and juice of one lemon
²/₃ cup/150mL/5fl oz heavy or
   whipping cream
18 oysters

METHOD

1. Toss the chicken in the flour, salt and black pepper and seal in a frying pan, a couple of pieces at a time. Remove to a large casserole. Fry the onions to soften, then add the garlic, mushrooms and sage. Add to the chicken. Deglaze the pan with the white wine and add it, with the water and lemon juice and zest, to the casserole.

2. Cover and bake in the oven, for 1¹/₂ hours at 350°F/180°C. Remove from the oven, add the cream and oysters and return to the oven for 15 minutes. Allow to rest for 10 minutes before giving it one last stir and serving. It should have thickened with the flour, but if it didn't, add a little cornstarch mixed with milk as you remove it from the oven.

Serves 4

Baked Oysters with Bacon

INGREDIENTS

1 clove garlic, crushed
3 tablespoons/45mL butter
2 cups/500mL fresh breadcrumbs
salt and pepper to taste
24 oysters (bottled or fresh)
3 bacon strips

METHOD

1. Preheat oven to 410°F/210°C.

2. Sauté garlic in butter 1–2 minutes. Add breadcrumbs, salt and pepper, and fry until just turning brown.

3. Drain oysters and place in a shallow, greased ovenproof dish.

4. Cover all over with browned crumbs, and place strips of bacon over top.

5. Put in hot oven until bacon is browned and crisp.

Serves 4

Coconut Prawns and Scallops

INGREDIENTS

2¼lb/1kg large uncooked prawns,
  shelled and deveined, tails intact

3 egg whites, lightly beaten

1 cup/250mL shredded coconut

vegetable oil for deep-frying

1 tablespoon/15mL peanut oil

4 fresh red chilies, seeded and sliced

2 small fresh green chilies, seeded
  and sliced

2 cloves garlic, crushed

1 tablespoon/15mL fresh ginger,
  grated

3 kaffir lime leaves, finely shredded

12oz/375g scallops

1½ cups/375mL snow pea leaves
  or sprouts

2 tablespoons/25mL palm or
  brown sugar

¼ cup/50mL lime juice

2 tablespoons/25mL Thai fish sauce
  (nam pla)

METHOD

1. Dip prawns in egg white, then roll in coconut to coat. Heat vegetable oil in a large saucepan until a cube of bread dropped in browns in 50 seconds. Cook prawns, a few at a time, for 2–3 minutes or until golden and crisp. Drain on paper towels and keep warm.

2. Heat peanut oil in a wok over a high heat, add red and green chilies, garlic, ginger and lime leaves and stir-fry for 2–3 minutes or until fragrant.

3. Add scallops to wok and stir-fry for 3 minutes or until opaque. Add cooked prawns, snow pea leaves, sugar, lime juice and fish sauce and stir-fry for 2 minutes or until heated.

Serves 6

Curried Scallops with Water Chestnuts

INGREDIENTS

1/2 cup/125mL chicken broth

1 teaspoon/5mL cornstarch

1 teaspoon/5mL fish sauce, or soy sauce

1/2 teaspoon/2mL cider vinegar

2 tablespoons/25mL light salad oil

1 small onion, chopped

2 tablespoons/25mL minced fresh ginger

2 cloves minced garlic

1 teaspoon/5mL curry powder

1/2 teaspoon/2mL ground coriander

1/2 teaspoon/2mL crushed red hot chili

12oz/375g sea scallops, rinsed and cut
   crosswise into 1/4in/5mm slices

8oz/227mL canned water chestnuts, ends
   trimmed and sliced (or use fresh)

2 tablespoons/25mL cilantro, chopped

METHOD

1. For sauce mixture: combine chicken broth, cornstarch, fish or soy sauce, and cider vinegar and set aside.

2. Place a medium-sized frying pan over medium high heat. Add oil, onion, ginger and garlic. Stir often until onion is tinged with brown (about 10 minutes). Add curry, coriander and chili and stir until curry becomes fragrant (about 1 minute).

3. Add scallops and water chestnuts and gently stir for 2 minutes until scallops are almost opaque throughout (cut to test), for 2 minutes. Add sauce mixture, and stir until it thickens. Pour onto a plate and sprinkle with cilantro.

Serves 2

Ginger Scallop Stir-Fry

INGREDIENTS

2 tablespoons/25mL fresh lime juice

2 tablespoons/25mL rice wine

1 clove garlic, crushed

8oz/250g bay scallops

1 tablespoon/15mL sesame oil

2 teaspoons/10mL fresh ginger,
 finely grated

4 green onions, cut diagonally into
 $1/2$ in/1cm lengths

$1^1/4$ cups/300mL button mushrooms,
 sliced

$1/2$ red bell pepper, diced

2 teaspoons/10mL soy sauce

pepper

1 teaspoon/5mL cornstarch

2 tablespoons/25mL water

METHOD

1. Combine the lime juice with the rice wine and crushed garlic. Marinate the scallops for 15 minutes. Set aside.

2. Heat the sesame oil in a hot wok or large skillet until almost smoking. Add the ginger, green onions, mushrooms and red bell pepper. Stir-fry for about 3 minutes, until the ginger has become fragrant.

3. Add the scallops and marinade. Continue stir-frying for another 3 minutes, until scallops have become opaque. Add the soy sauce and mix thoroughly. Add pepper to taste.

4. Make a slurry of the cornstarch and water. Drizzle the slurry into the wok. Cook for another minute or two or until the sauce has thickened and become smooth. Serve immediately with steamed white rice.

Serves 4

Coquilles Saint-Jacques en Seviche
(Scallops Marinated in Citrus Juices)

INGREDIENTS

1lb/500g sea or bay scallops

juice of 2 limes

juice of 1 orange

grated rind of 1 lemon,
   1 lime, 1/2 orange

salt and freshly cracked pepper to
   taste

2 tablespoons/25mL orange
   liqueur

4–6 lime slices

1 head lettuce, your choice

METHOD

1. Slice the raw scallops thinly. Mix all ingredients, except the lettuce and add the scallops. Let sit covered in the refrigerator overnight. (The acid in the citrus juice will cook the scallops.)

2. To serve, arrange your favorite lettuce on cold plates, and top with a mound of the scallops.

3. Garnish with a slice of lime. This recipe should be made one day prior to serving.

Serves 4–6

Baked Oysters

INGREDIENTS

3 tablespoons/45mL butter

3 1/2 cups/875mL fresh breadcrumbs

1 teaspoon/5mL freshly crushed garlic

1 tablespoon/15mL fresh chopped parsley

2 dozen fresh oysters

2/3 cup/150mL Parmesan cheese (freshly
   grated)

2 tablespoons/25mL butter (extra)

METHOD

1. Preheat oven to 410°F/210°C.

2. Grease an ovenproof platter (just large enough to hold the oysters in a single layer).

3. Melt butter in a frypan over a moderate heat. When the foam subsides, add the breadcrumbs and garlic and toss (until golden). Stir in the parsley.

4. Spread about two-thirds of the breadcrumb mixture in the bottom of the platter and arrange the oysters over it.

5. Mix the rest of the breadcrumbs with the grated cheese and spread over the oysters.

6. Dot the top with the extra butter chopped into tiny pieces.

7. Bake in the preheated hot oven for 15 minutes (or until top is golden).

Serves 6–8

Ginger Scallops

INGREDIENTS

1 tablespoon/15mL peanut oil

2 teaspoons/10mL minced fresh
   ginger

1 clove minced garlic

1¹/2 cups/375mL whole snow peas,
   fresh or frozen

1 cup/250mL carrots, thinly sliced

1lb/500g sea scallops

1 tablespoon/15mL light soy sauce

¹/8 teaspoon/1mL salt

2 teaspoons/10mL cornstarch

¹/4 cup/50mL sliced green onions

2 cups/500mL hot cooked rice

METHOD

1. Heat oil in wok over medium-high heat and add ginger and garlic. Stir-fry for 30 seconds. Add snow peas and carrots and stir-fry a couple of minutes.

2. Remove vegetables from wok, set aside and keep warm. Add scallops to wok and cook over medium-high heat about 3 minutes, or until scallops are cooked, stirring constantly.

3. Combine soy sauce, salt and cornstarch, stir well and add to the wok. Add green onions and cook 1 minute, stirring constantly. Add vegetables and serve over hot rice.

Serves 4

Griddled Scallops with Orange Salsa

INGREDIENTS

2 small oranges

4 sun-dried tomatoes in oil,
drained and chopped

1 clove garlic, crushed

1 tablespoon/15mL balsamic vinegar

4 tablespoons/60mL extra virgin olive oil

salt and black pepper

1 large head fennel, cut lengthwise into
8 slices

12 fresh scallops

4 tablespoons/60mL crème fraîche
(see page 12)

arugula leaves to serve

METHOD

1. Slice the top and bottom off one of the oranges, then cut away the peel and pith, following the curve of the fruit. Cut between the membranes to release the segments, then chop roughly. Squeeze the juice of the other orange into a bowl, add the chopped orange, tomatoes, garlic, vinegar and 3 tablespoons/45mL of the oil, then season.

2. Heat a ridged cast-iron grill pan or heavy-based frying pan. Brush both sides of each fennel slice with half the remaining oil. Cook for 2—3 minutes on each side, until tender and charred. Transfer to serving plates and keep warm.

3. Cook scallops in the remaining oil for 1 minute, then turn and cook for 30 seconds or until cooked through. Divide fennel into 4 servings and top each with 1 tablespoon/15mL of crème fraîche, 3 scallops and the salsa. Serve with the arugula.

Serves 4

Creamed Oysters

INGREDIENTS

1 large jar oysters

2 tablespoons/25mL butter

2 tablespoons/25mL all-purpose flour

1 cup/250mL milk

1/3 cup/75mL cream

pinch cayenne pepper

2 tablespoons/25mL dry sherry

salt to taste

4 slices hot, buttered toast

chopped parsley, to garnish

METHOD

1. Drain oysters (reserving 1/4 cup/50mL liquid).

2. Melt butter in saucepan, stir in flour, and cook (for 2 minutes) over low heat.

3. Slowly stir in milk, cream and reserved oyster liquid. Add cayenne pepper, sherry and salt (to taste). Simmer for 2 minutes.

4. Add oysters, and simmer another minute or two (until oysters are just plump).

5. Spoon over toast and sprinkle with parsley.

Serves 4

Scallop and Mango Sangchssajang

INGREDIENTS

21oz/600g scallops

1 tablespoon/15mL cornstarch

2 teaspoons/10mL brown sugar

2 teaspoons/10mL olive or peanut oil

2 shallots, thinly sliced

1 tablespoon/15mL fresh ginger, grated

6 spears fresh asparagus, chopped

1/2 cup/125mL rice wine (mirin) or dry
   white wine

2 tablespoons/25mL lime or lemon juice

2 teaspoons/10mL fish sauce, optional

2 teaspoons/10mL reduced-salt soy sauce

few drops chili sauce or 1 small fresh red
   chili, thinly sliced

1 mango, flesh diced

2 tablespoons/25mL fresh sweet basil or
   cilantro, shredded

1 1/2 cups/375mL hot cooked jasmine or
   calrose rice

1 head butter lettuce or radicchio,
   leaves separated

METHOD

1. Place scallops, cornstarch and sugar in a plastic food bag. Toss gently to coat.

2. Heat 1 teaspoon/5mL of the oil in a non-stick frying pan over a high heat. Add scallops. Stir-fry for 2—3 minutes or until scallops are just cooked. Remove scallops from pan. Set aside.

3. Heat remaining oil in pan. Add shallots and ginger. Stir-fry for 1 minute or until soft.

4. Add asparagus, wine, lime juice and fish, soy and chili sauces. Stir-fry for 4 minutes or until the asparagus is tender. Add mango and basil. Toss to combine.

5. To serve, spoon rice into lettuce cups, then spoon in some of the scallop mixture. To eat, fold lettuce around scallops and eat in your hands.

Serves 4 as a light meal or 6 as a starter

PASTA WITH SCALLOPS, ZUCCHINI AND TOMATOES

Pasta with Scallops, Zucchini and Tomatoes

INGREDIENTS

1lb/455g dry fettucine pasta

1/4 cup/50mL olive oil

3 cloves garlic, minced

2 zucchinis, diced

1/2 teaspoon/2mL salt

1/2 teaspoon/2mL crushed red pepper flakes

4 Roma tomatoes, chopped

1lb/500g bay scallops

1 cup/250mL chopped fresh basil, optional

2 tablespoons/25mL grated Parmesan cheese

METHOD

1. Cook pasta in a large pot with boiling salted water until al dente. Drain.

2. Meanwhile, heat oil in a large skillet, add garlic and cook until tender. Add the zucchini, salt, red pepper flakes, and sauté for 10 minutes. Add chopped tomatoes, bay scallops, and fresh basil (if using) and simmer for 5 minutes, or until scallops are opaque.

3. Pour sauce over cooked pasta and serve with grated Parmesan cheese.

Serves 4—6

Scallops with Vegetables

INGREDIENTS

1 teaspoon/5mL cornstarch

1 tablespoon/15mL water

1 teaspoon/5mL soy sauce

1/2 teaspoon/2mL sugar

3/4 cup/175mL green beans

1 tablespoon/15mL oil (approx.)

9oz/250g scallops

1 white onion, thinly sliced

11/2 cups/375mL mushrooms, sliced

3/4 cup/175mL celery, sliced

1/2 cup/125mL bamboo shoots, thinly sliced

4oz/114mL canned pineapple pieces,
   drained

1 cup/250mL chicken stock

METHOD

1. Mix together cornstarch, water, soy sauce and sugar.

2. Drop beans into boiling water, and cook for 3–4 minutes.

3. Heat about 1 tablespoon/15mL oil, and add scallops. Fry for 1 minute, stirring constantly. Remove scallops from pan.

4. Add onion, mushrooms, celery and bamboo shoots. Stir-fry for another 3 minutes. Add pineapple pieces, stock and beans. Cook over medium heat for 2 minutes.

5. Add scallops. Stir the cornstarch mixture, add to pan, and cook, stirring, for 2 minutes.

Serves 4

Pasta with Pesto and Scallops

INGREDIENTS

1lb/500g dry fettucine pasta

$^1/_4$ cup/50mL pesto sauce

2 tablespoons/25mL olive oil

$^1/_2$ onion, chopped

2 cloves garlic, minced

3 tablespoons/45mL olive oil

1 green bell pepper, thinly sliced

$^1/_2$ cup/125mL fresh sliced mushrooms

2 tablespoons/25mL dry white wine

2 tablespoons/25mL lemon juice

salt to taste

ground black pepper to taste

1lb/500g scallops

2 tablespoons/25mL grated
  Parmesan cheese

METHOD

1. Cook pasta in a large pot with boiling salted water until al dente. Drain. Stir in pesto sauce and 2 tablespoons/25mL of olive oil.

2. Meanwhile, in a large skillet, sauté onion and garlic in olive oil until soft. Add green bell pepper and mushrooms and cook for 3 minutes, or until soft. Stir in dry white wine, lemon juice, salt and pepper to taste, and bring to a boil. Add scallops and toss for 2 minutes. Take care not to overcook the scallops, as they will toughen when exposed to prolonged heat.

3. Toss the pesto-covered pasta with the scallop sauce. Sprinkle with grated Parmesan cheese. Serve immediately.

Serves 4—6

Oyster Casserole

INGREDIENTS

6 tablespoons/90mL oil

1/2 small onion, sliced

1 1/2 cups/375mL fresh mushrooms, sliced

4 tablespoons/60mL all-purpose flour

1 teaspoon/5mL salt

1 teaspoon/5mL paprika

pinch cayenne

2 cups/500mL milk

2 dozen raw oysters, with their juice

3 hard-boiled eggs, sliced

2 tablespoons/25mL cooking sherry

METHOD

1. Heat oil, add onions and mushrooms. Cook until tender and remove from pan. Blend flour with oil lining the pan. Add seasonings, fry for 2 minutes then add milk gradually.

2. Cook oysters in their own liquor until edges curl. Add oysters and liquor to mixture. Add mushrooms, onion and eggs, then stir in sherry. Turn into greased casserole and bake at 400°F/200°C for 15 minutes. Serve on toast or pastry shells.

Serves 4

Sauté of Scallops

INGREDIENTS

2 tablespoons/25mL butter

1 large onion, chopped

2 teaspoons/10mL freshly crushed garlic

24oz/680g scallops

3 tablespoons/45mL all-purpose flour

1 teaspoon/5mL Madras curry powder

pepper and salt

1 cup/250mL milk

chopped parsley, for garnish

METHOD

1. In a large pan, melt the butter. Sauté onion and garlic until onion is soft.

2. Beard scallops, rinse well and dry. Toss in flour mixed with curry powder, pepper and salt.

3. Sauté scallops in pan with garlic and onion until scallops are golden. Stir in milk.

4. Bring mixture to boil, then simmer for a few minutes or until scallops are just tender.

5. Sprinkle with chopped parsley to serve.

Serves 5–6

Oysters Marinated with Bacon

INGREDIENTS

2 tablespoons/25mL soy sauce

$^1/_2$ teaspoon/2mL Worcestershire sauce

1 tablespoon/15mL honey

4 strips rindless back bacon,
    cut into $1^1/_4$ in/3cm strips

2 dozen oysters

12 small wooden skewers

METHOD

1. In a small bowl combine soy sauce, Worcestershire sauce and honey and set aside.

2. Wrap a bacon strip around each oyster, then thread 2 wrapped oysters onto each skewer. Place skewers in a foil-lined grill pan. Pour marinade over oysters, cover and leave for 30 minutes.

3. Cook oysters under a preheated grill until bacon is golden. Serve immediately.

Makes 12

Grilled Scallops with Salsa

INGREDIENTS

Pineapple Salsa

1 cup/250mL chopped pineapple

1/4 red bell pepper, finely chopped

2 medium green chilies, chopped

1 tablespoon/15mL cilantro, chopped

1 tablespoon/15mL fresh mint leaves, chopped

1 tablespoon/15mL lime juice

30 scallops

chili or lime oil

crisp tortilla chips

METHOD

1. To make salsa, place pineapple, red bell pepper, chilies, cilantro, mint and lime juice in a bowl. Toss to combine, then stand for 20 minutes.

2. Brush scallops with oil and cook on a preheated hot grill or barbecue plate (griddle) for 30 seconds on each side or until scallops just change color. Serve immediately with salsa and tortilla chips.

Serves 4

Scallop Casserole

INGREDIENTS

1lb/500g scallops, fresh or frozen

1/4 cup/50mL chopped onions

1 can (14oz/398mL) cream of mushroom soup

1/2 cup/125mL milk

1/2 –1 tsp/2-5mL curry powder

1/4 teaspoon/1mL pepper

1 cup/250mL grated cheese

1 bunch asparagus, cut into 2in/4cm lengths

2 tablespoons/25mL melted butter

1 cup/250mL bread cubes

parsley

lemon rind, grated

METHOD

1. Thaw scallops if frozen. Wash scallops and drain well. Simmer scallops in boiling water. Drain. Sauté onions. Add soup, milk, curry, pepper and half of the cheese. Stir until cheese melts.

2. Slice scallops and add to soup mix along with asparagus. Add bread cubes that have been dipped in melted butter. Sprinkle with remaining cheese. Bake in 425°F/215°C oven for 15 minutes or until golden.

3. Remove from oven and sprinkle with chopped parsley and lemon rind prior to serving

Serves 4

Creamed Scallops

INGREDIENTS

24oz/680g scallops

1 cup/250mL dry white wine

1/2 cup/125mL water

1 teaspoon/5mL lemon juice

1 tablespoon/15mL butter

1 tablespoon/15mL all-purpose flour

1 cup/250mL milk

1/2 cup/125mL cream

salt and pepper

pinch cayenne pepper

6 deep scallop shells

1 cup/250mL cheese, grated

METHOD

1. Poach scallops in wine, water and lemon juice for 3–4 minutes. Cool, strain off liquid, and reserve.

2. Melt butter, add flour and cook, stirring, for 2 minutes. Gradually stir in the reserved liquid and milk. Stir until boiling.

3. Cook rapidly for 4–5 minutes. Add cream and boil again, until thick. Season with salt, pepper and cayenne pepper.

4. Add scallops and spoon into 6 deep scallop shells. Sprinkle with cheese.

5. Brown under grill.

Serves 4–6

Garlic Scallops

INGREDIENTS

1 medium-sized onion, diced finely

4—6 cloves garlic, finely chopped

1 tablespoon/15mL olive oil

1lb/500g scallops

1/4 cup/50mL/2fl oz white wine

1/2 cup/125mL/3 1/2 fl oz light cream

4 green onions, sliced on an angle

rice pilaf for serving

1 tablespoon/15mL finely chopped
    chives or parsley

METHOD

1. Fry onion and garlic with oil in a medium hot pan for 2 minutes, but don't allow to color. Add scallops and lightly cook on one side for 20 seconds. Turn scallops over and cook for another 20 seconds and then remove from pan.

2. On medium to high heat, add the splash of white wine to pan and reduce for 1 minute. Add cream and reduce until the sauce thickens.

3. Add scallops, green onions and gently toss in sauce for about 1 minute. Place scallops on big mound of rice pilaf, pour the sauce over, then garnish with chives or parsley.

Serves 4–6

Note: This lovely dish can be enlarged by the addition of prawns and/or fillets of fish.

Scallops with Plum Glaze

INGREDIENTS

24oz/680g scallops

8 bamboo skewers

3 tablespoons/45mL plum sauce

1 1/2 tablespoons/20mL lemon juice

1/2 teaspoon/2mL lemon rind, grated

sprinkling lemon pepper seasoning

METHOD

1. Wash and clean scallops. Thread evenly onto 8 skewers.

2. Combine plum sauce, lemon juice, lemon rind and lemon pepper. Stir well to combine.

3. Place scallops under grill and baste with sauce mixture. Turn once.

4. Cook for a minute or less on each side.

Serves 4–6

Scallop Quiche

INGREDIENTS

1¹/₂lb/750g scallops (cut large scallops
   in half)

2 tablespoons/25mL vermouth

2 tablespoons/25mL minced parsley
   or chives

¹/₄ teaspoon/1mL dried thyme

salt and pepper

9in/23cm pastry pie crust

5 eggs, beaten

1 cup/250mL light cream

¹/₄–¹/₂ red bell pepper, thinly julienned

paprika

METHOD

1. Preheat oven to 450°F/230°C. In a bowl,
mix scallops, vermouth, parsley or chives,
thyme, salt and pepper. Fill pie crust with
scallop mixture. In a separate bowl,
mix eggs and cream then pour over scallop
mixture.

2. Arrange red bell pepper slices on top and
sprinkle with paprika. Bake for 10 minutes.
Lower heat to 350°F/180°C and continue
baking for 25–30 minutes until done. To check
if quiche is cooked, insert a knife into center.
If knife comes out clean, quiche is done.

Serves 6

Spaghettini and Scallops with Breadcrumbs

INGREDIENTS

12 fresh scallops, with corals (roe)

1/2 cup/125mL/4fl oz extra virgin olive oil

1/2 cup/125mL dried white breadcrumbs

4 tablespoons/60mL chopped fresh
  flat-leaf parsley

2 cloves garlic, finely chopped

1 teaspoon/5mL crushed dried chilies

12oz/375g dried spaghettini

4 tablespoons/60mL dry white wine

METHOD

1. Detach the corals from the scallops and set aside. Slice the white part of each scallop into 3 or 4 pieces. Heat 2 tablespoons/25mL of oil in a frying pan, then add the breadcrumbs and fry, stirring, for 3 minutes or until golden. Remove from the pan and set aside.

2. Heat 5 tablespoons/75mL of oil in the pan, then add half the parsley and the garlic and chili and fry for 2 minutes or until the flavors are released. Meanwhile, cook pasta in plenty of boiling salted water, until al dente. Drain, return to the saucepan and toss with remaining oil.

3. Stir-fry the white parts of the scallops for 30 seconds or until they are starting to turn opaque. Add wine and reserved scallop corals and cook for 30 seconds. Add spaghettini and cook for 1 minute, tossing to combine. Sprinkle with breadcrumbs and remaining parsley.

Serves 4

Scallop Seviche

INGREDIENTS

1¹/₂ teaspoons/7mL ground cumin

1 cup/250mL fresh lime juice

¹/₂ cup/125mL fresh orange juice

2lb/1kg bay scallops

1 hot red chili pepper

¹/₄ cup/50mL red onion, finely chopped

3 ripe plum tomatoes, chopped

1 red bell pepper, seeded and chopped

3 green onions, chopped

1 cup/250mL cilantro, chopped

1 lime, sliced, for garnish

METHOD

1. Stir the cumin into the lime and orange juice and pour over the scallops.

2. Stir in the chopped chili pepper and red onion. Cover and refrigerate for at least 2 hours.

3. Just before serving, drain the scallops and mix with the chopped tomatoes, bell pepper, green onions and cilantro. Garnish with the slices of lime.

Serves 4

Note: Hot red chili pepper should be finely chopped. Plum tomatoes should be seeded and chopped.

Simple Scallops

INGREDIENTS

2 tablespoons/25mL olive oil

1 clove garlic

1lb/500g scallops, with their liquid

1 teaspoon/5mL dried thyme

¹/₈ teaspoon/1mL red pepper flakes

¹/₄ cup/50mL white wine

METHOD

1. Heat olive oil in large pan or skillet. (Pan should be large enough to hold scallops in one layer.) Peel the garlic clove and cut into four pieces. Drain scallops and reserve the liquid.

2. Add thyme, pepper flakes and garlic to the hot oil. Simmer gently for 3–4 minutes to roast the spices. Remove the garlic pieces if they turn brown.

3. Add white wine and scallop juice to pan. Cover and simmer 10 minutes to develop flavors.

4. Add scallops to the pan. Cover and simmer until done, about 5 minutes. Turn a couple of times.

5. Scallops are cooked when they just begin to offer some resistance to the touch. If cooked too long, they toughen.

Serves 4

Note: Scallops are just fine braised with a little thyme and white wine. Our version goes a bit further, using classic Mediterranean flavors of thyme, red pepper flakes and garlic roasted in olive oil to complement the scallop flavor. Braised scallops can be held indefinitely. If refrigerated for over half an hour, reheat gently in the microwave.

Scallops and Wilted Spinach

INGREDIENTS

6oz/170g package baby spinach leaves
  (or about 4 cups/1L lightly packed)
2 teaspoons/10mL sesame seeds
2 tablespoons/25mL soy sauce
1 tablespoon/15mL lemon juice
2 teaspoons/10mL sesame oil
18 scallops
vegetable oil
crushed black peppercorns

METHOD

1. Preheat barbecue to a medium heat.

2. To make salad, blanch spinach leaves in boiling water for 10 seconds. Drain spinach, refresh under cold running water, drain again and place in a bowl.

3. Place sesame seeds, soy sauce, lemon juice and sesame oil in a bowl and mix to combine. Spoon dressing over spinach and toss to combine. Divide salad among 6 serving plates.

4. Place scallops in bowl, drizzle with a little vegetable oil and season to taste with black pepper. Sear scallops on barbecue plate (griddle) for 45–60 seconds or until golden and flesh is opaque. Place scallops on top of each portion of salad and serve immediately.

Serves 6

Note: Alternatively the scallops can be seared in a hot frying pan.

Cajun Seafood Pasta

INGREDIENTS

1lb/500g dry fettucine pasta

2 cups/500mL heavy or whipping cream

1 tablespoon/15mL fresh basil, chopped

1 tablespoon/15mL fresh thyme, chopped

2 teaspoons/10mL salt

2 teaspoons/10mL ground black pepper

1½ teaspoons/7mL crushed red
    pepper flakes

1 teaspoon/5mL ground white pepper

1 cup/250mL green onions, chopped

1 cup/250mL parsley, chopped

8oz/250g prawns, peeled and deveined

8oz/250g scallops

½ cup/125mL Swiss cheese, grated

½ cup/125mL grated Parmesan cheese

METHOD

1. Cook pasta in a large pot of boiling salted water until al dente.

2. Meanwhile, pour cream into large skillet. Cook over medium heat, stirring constantly, until nearly boiling. Reduce heat, and add herbs, salt, peppers, onions and parsley. Simmer 7–8 minutes, or until thickened.

3. Stir in seafood, cooking until prawns are no longer transparent. Stir in cheeses, blending well.

4. Drain pasta. Pour sauce over pasta.

Serves 4–6

Scallop Thermidor

INGREDIENTS

1¹/₄ cups/300mL button mushrooms, quartered

¹/₄ cup/50mL butter or margarine, melted

¹/₄ cup/50mL all-purpose flour

1 teaspoon/5mL salt

¹/₂ teaspoon/2mL dry mustard

2 cups/500mL milk

1lb/500g cooked scallops

2 tablespoons/25mL parsley or chives, chopped

pinch cayenne pepper

Parmesan cheese (grated)

paprika

METHOD

1. Sauté mushrooms in butter for 5 minutes then stir in flour and seasonings.

2. Add milk gradually and cook until thick, stirring constantly.

3. Add scallops, parsley or chives and cayenne pepper.

4. Place in 6 well buttered shells or 5oz/150mL custard cups.

5. Sprinkle with cheese and paprika.

6. Bake at 400°F/200°C for 10–15 minutes, until cheese is browned.

Serves 6

Scallop Stir-Fry

INGREDIENTS

1 tablespoon/15mL olive oil

3–4 drops sesame oil

1 medium-sized onion, finely sliced

2 cloves garlic, crushed

1 teaspoon/5mL fresh ginger,
   finely chopped

1 small red bell pepper, sliced

1 small green bell pepper, sliced

1 cup/250mL broccoli florets

1/2 cup/125mL bean sprout shoots

4 green onions, sliced

1lb/500g scallops, cut on an angle

1 tablespoon/15mL oyster sauce

1 tablespoon/15mL light soy sauce

1 fresh chili or 1 teaspoon/5mL of
   chili sauce

11/2 cups/375mL of water, thickened with
   2 teaspoons/10mL cornstarch

20 cilantro leaves (optional)

METHOD

1. Heat oils in wok or frying pan, add onion, garlic and ginger and stir-fry over medium heat for 30 seconds. Add bell peppers, broccoli, sprouts and green onions and stir-fry a further 2 minutes on high heat.

2. Add scallops and sauces and stir-fry for 1 minute. Add cornstarch water and stir until mixture thickens.

3. Toss in cilantro, if desired, and serve with boiled rice.

Serves 4

Scallops Fenton

INGREDIENTS

1¹/2 cups/375mL dry white wine

2 tablespoons/25mL fresh lemon juice

3lb/1¹/3 kg scallops

3 cups/750mL mushrooms, sliced

1 small green bell pepper, sliced

¹/4 cup/50mL butter

¹/2 teaspoon/2mL salt

pinch freshly ground pepper

4 tablespoons/60mL all-purpose flour

1 cup/250mL diced Swiss cheese

¹/2 cup/125mL grated Romano cheese

1 cup/250mL heavy cream, whipped

2 tablespoons/25mL butter for topping

paprika

METHOD

1. Bring wine and lemon juice to boil and add scallops, mushrooms and green bell pepper. Simmer until scallops are just tender. Be careful not to overcook. Drain, reserving liquid. Melt butter in saucepan then blend in salt, pepper, and flour until bubbly. Gradually stir in reserved liquid and cook until thickened.

2. Add Swiss cheese and half of the Romano and stir over very low heat until blended. Remove from heat and fold in whipped cream.

3. Stir in scallop mixture, then divide among 8 individual buttered scallop shells/baking dishes. Sprinkle tops with remaining Romano, dot with butter and sprinkle with paprika. Place under broiler or grill and cook until golden brown.

Serves 8

Scallops with Snow Peas and Corn

INGREDIENTS

12oz/340g fresh or frozen sea scallops

²/3 cup/150mL water

2 tablespoons/25mL dry sherry

1 tablespoon/15mL cornstarch

2 teaspoons/10mL soy sauce

1 teaspoon/5mL grated fresh ginger

¹/2 teaspoon/2mL instant chicken
    stock granules

1 tablespoon/15mL cooking oil

2 cups/500mL fresh snow peas, strings
    removed (or frozen and thawed)

1 cup/250mL frozen whole baby sweet
    corn, thawed (or canned and drained)

16 cherry tomatoes, cut into quarters

3 green onions, sliced (¹/3 cup/75mL)

2 cups/500mL hot cooked ramen or other
    fine noodles

METHOD

1. Thaw scallops, if frozen. Cut any large scallops in half and set aside.

2. For sauce, stir together water, sherry, cornstarch, soy sauce, ginger and stock granules in a small bowl. Set aside.

3. Pour cooking oil into a wok or large skillet. (Add more oil as necessary during cooking.) Preheat over medium-high heat. Stir-fry fresh snow peas (add frozen in step 5) and corn in hot oil for 1–2 minutes or until crisp-tender. Remove vegetables from the wok.

4. Add scallops to the hot wok. Stir-fry for 2 minutes or until scallops turn opaque. Push scallops from the center of the wok.

5. Stir sauce and pour into the center of the wok. Cook and stir until thickened and bubbly. Return cooked vegetables to the wok. Add thawed frozen snow peas (if using), tomatoes and green onions. Stir all ingredients together to coat with sauce. Cook and stir 1–2 minutes more or until heated through. Serve immediately over hot cooked noodles.

Serves 4

Scallops Tarragon

INGREDIENTS

1lb/500g mixed or jumbo scallops,
   fresh or frozen
2 tablespoons/25mL butter or
   margarine
1/4 cup/50mL sliced green onion
1 cup/250mL sugar snap peas
1/4 teaspoon/2mL dried tarragon,
   crushed
1 tablespoon/15mL dry white wine
freshly ground black pepper
hot cooked rice

METHOD

1. Thaw the scallops if frozen. Make sure to cut jumbo scallops in half.

2. Rinse and pat dry with paper towels.

3. In a skillet, heat butter or margarine over medium-high heat. Add the green onion and stir-fry for 1 minute. Then push the onion to one side.

4. Add scallops, sugar snap peas and tarragon. Cook stirring frequently for 5-6 minutes or until scallops are opaque and most of the liquid has evaporated.

5. Stir in white wine and sprinkle with freshly ground black pepper. Serve with hot cooked rice.

Serves 2

Braised Scallops with Peas, Ham and Onion Sauce

INGREDIENTS

1/2 cup/125mL frozen peas
1 teaspoon/5mL sugar
1 clove garlic
1lb/500g scallops with their liquid
3 tablespoons/45mL olive oil
1/2 teaspoon/2mL dried thyme
red chili flakes to taste
3/4 cup/175mL onions,
   chopped coarsely
2 tablespoons/25mL ham, cooked
   and diced
1/3 cup/75mL white wine and
   scallop juice (combined)
1/3 cup/75mL water, more if needed
cornstarch, 1 teaspoon/5mL per cup
   of liquids, mixed in a little water
   (optional)

METHOD

1. Set frozen peas in a bowl to thaw at room temperature. Sprinkle in sugar. (To thaw quickly, place in a pan with a tablespoon of water. Heat covered a couple of minutes.)

2. Peel the garlic clove and cut into four pieces. Drain the scallops and reserve liquid.

3. Warm olive oil in sauté pan, or skillet, with cover large enough to hold scallops in one layer. Add thyme, chili flakes and garlic. Simmer gently 3 or 4 minutes to roast the spices. Remove the garlic pieces if they become brown at any point.

4. Add chopped onion and ham. Cook until the onions soften (about 5 minutes).

5. Add white wine, scallop juice and water to pan. Cover and simmer 10 minutes to develop flavors. Add spoonfuls of water if running dry.

6. Add scallops to the pan. Cover and simmer for about 5 minutes. Turn a couple of times.

7. Scallops are done when they just begin to offer some resistance to the touch. If cooked too long, they toughen.

8. If thickening is desired add cornstarch and water.

Serves 4

Scallops with Zucchini in Apple Butter

INGREDIENTS

2 zucchini, cut into 1in/2¹/₂ cm slices

8 large scallops with corals (roe)

1 tablespoon/15mL olive oil

salt and black pepper

¹/₂ cup/125mL apple juice

2 tablespoons/25mL butter

fresh flat-leaf parsley to garnish

METHOD

1. Coat the zucchini slices and scallops gently in the oil and season.

2. Heat a large heavy-based frying pan until hot, add the zucchini slices and cook for 2 minutes on one side. Turn the zucchini over and add the scallops to the pan. Cook for 1 minute, then turn the scallops over. Cook for a further minute, until the scallops are golden and the zucchinis are browned.

3. Remove the scallops and zucchini slices from the pan and keep warm. Pour the apple juice into the pan, add the butter and cook until reduced to a syrupy sauce. Spoon the sauce over the scallops and zucchini slices and garnish with parsley.

Serves 4

Baked Scallops

INGREDIENTS

1 can cream of mushroom soup

2/3 cup/150mL milk

1 1/2 cups/375mL cracker crumbs

**3/4 teaspoon/4mL each of garlic powder,
oregano and thyme**

1lb/500g bay scallops

paprika

METHOD

1. Preheat oven to 375°F/190°C. In a
9in/23cm round dish, mix soup with milk and
set aside. Break up the crackers and mix
with the spices. Using 1/3 of the spice
mixture, coat each of the scallops, then place
them in dish with soup mixture. Sprinkle
remaining spice mixture over the top of the
scallops. Sprinkle paprika over the top and
bake for 30–35 minutes.

2. You may put the dish under the broiler for
a couple of minutes to create a light crust on
top. Serve with rice. Good with a green
vegetable and salad.

Serves 4

Scallops with White Butter Sauce

INGREDIENTS

1½lb/750g scallops
salt and freshly ground pepper
1½ cups/375mL white wine
a little lemon juice
¾ cup/175mL snow peas or thinly sliced
    green beans
1 tablespoon/15mL green onion, chopped
½ cup/125mL butter, cut in pieces
a few chives to garnish

METHOD

1. Remove any beards from the scallops then wash. Carefully remove the roes and lay on paper towels to dry. Season with salt and pepper. Poach the scallops and roes in wine and lemon juice for approximately 2 minutes. Remove and keep warm.

2. String snow peas or green beans and drop into boiling salted water for 1 minute then drain. Add the green onion to the poaching liquid and reduce to about ½ cup/125mL. Over a gentle heat, add butter a little at a time, whisking it in to make a sauce the consistency of pouring cream.

3. Garnish with chives. Serve with crusty bread to mop up the lovely sauce.

Serves 4

Scallop or Prawn Curry

INGREDIENTS

1 cup/250mL onion, chopped
1 whole apple, peeled and chopped
2 cloves garlic, minced
1 tablespoon/15mL curry powder
2 tablespoons/25mL butter or margarine
¼ cup/50mL all-purpose flour
½ teaspoon/2mL salt
¼ teaspoon/1mL cardamom
¼ teaspoon/1mL pepper, freshly ground
1¼ cups/300mL nonfat chicken broth
1 tablespoon/15mL lime juice, fresh
1¼ lb/625g scallops or prawns
1 cup/250mL mushrooms, thinly sliced

METHOD

1. In a large skillet, sauté onion, apple, garlic and curry powder in butter or margarine until tender.

2. Remove skillet from heat and blend in flour, salt, cardamom and pepper. Stir in chicken broth and lime juice until curry sauce is well blended. Bring curry sauce to a boil, reduce heat and simmer uncovered for about 5 minutes, stirring occasionally.

3. Meanwhile, place scallops or prawns in a pot of boiling water and cook for 5 minutes or until just tender. Drain and set aside.

4. When curry sauce is finished cooking, add shellfish and mushrooms and serve over rice.

Serves 4

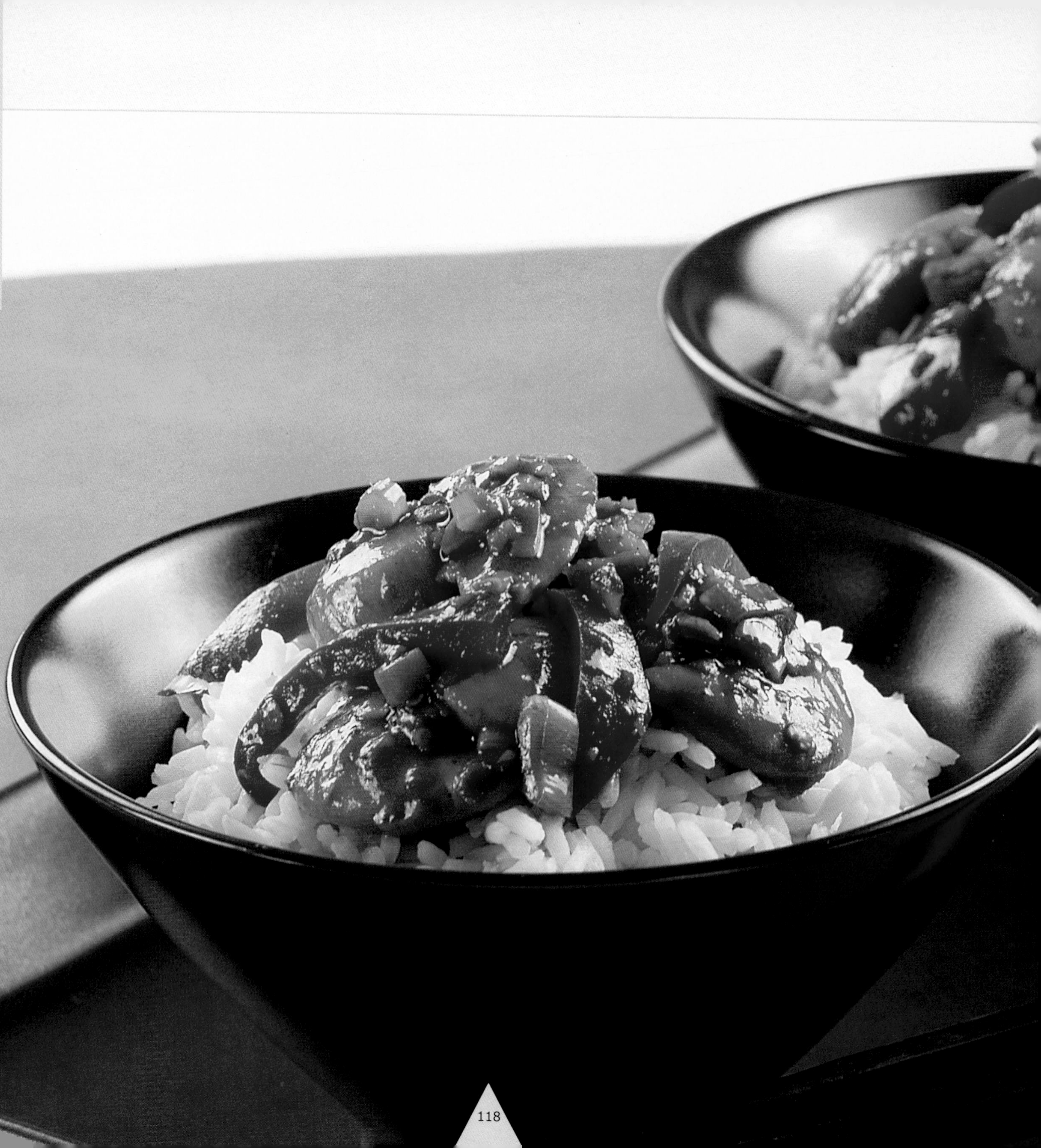

Sichuan-Style Scallops

INGREDIENTS

1¹/₂ tablespoons/20mL peanut oil

1 tablespoon/15mL fresh ginger,
   finely chopped

1 tablespoon/15mL garlic, finely chopped

2 tablespoons/25mL green onion,
   finely chopped

1lb/500g scallops, including corals (roe)

Sauce

1 tablespoon/15mL rice wine or dry sherry

2 teaspoons/10mL light soy sauce

2 teaspoons/10mL dark soy sauce

2 tablespoons/25mL chili bean sauce

2 teaspoons/10mL tomato puree

1 teaspoon/5mL sugar

¹/₂ teaspoon/2mL salt

¹/₂ teaspoon/2mL sugar

2 teaspoons/10mL sesame oil

plain rice for serving

METHOD

1. Heat wok until very hot. Add the oil and when it is very hot add the ginger, garlic and green onions. Stir-fry for 10 seconds. Add the scallops and stir-fry for 1 minute.

2. Add all the sauce ingredients except the sesame oil. Stir fry for 4 minutes, or until the scallops are firm and thoroughly coated with the sauce.

3. Add the sesame oil and stir-fry for another minute. Serve at once with plain rice.

Serves 4

Steak and Oyster Pot Pie

INGREDIENTS

Ricotta Pastry

1 cups self-rising flour
1/4 cup/125mL low-fat ricotta cheese
1/4 cup/125mL buttermilk
1/2 egg white
1 tablespoon/15mL unsaturated oil
1 tablespoon/15mL chilled skim milk

1 1/2 lb/680g lean round or topside steak,
   trimmed of visible fat and diced
1/2 cup/125mL all-purpose flour, seasoned
   with black pepper
1 tablespoon/15mL olive oil
1 onion, diced
1 large carrot, chopped
1 parsnip, chopped
2 stalks celery, chopped
1/4 cup/50mL tomato paste
1 cup/250mL red wine
1 cup/250mL beef stock
1/2 cup/125mL strong coffee
1 teaspoon/5mL Worcestershire sauce
12 fresh oysters or 2 x 3oz/85g canned
   smoked oysters, rinsed and drained
3 tablespoons/45mL fresh parsley,
   chopped
2 tablespoons/25mL cornstarch blended
   with 1/4 cup/50mL water

METHOD

Ricotta Pastry

1. Place flour, ricotta cheese, buttermilk, egg white and oil in food processor. Using the pulse button, process until just combined.

2. With machine running, slowly add skim milk until mixture forms a dough.

3. Turn pastry onto a lightly floured surface. Knead into a ball. Wrap pastry in plastic food wrap. Refrigerate for at least 30 minutes or until ready to use.

Pie Filling

1. Place meat and flour in a plastic food bag. Toss to coat.

2. Heat half the oil in a large non-stick frying pan over a medium heat. Add onion, carrot, parsnip and celery. Cook, stirring, for 3 minutes or until vegetables are soft. Remove vegetables from pan. Set aside.

3. Add remaining oil to pan and heat. Shake excess flour from meat. Add meat to pan. Cook, turning several times, until brown on all sides. Stir in tomato paste and cook for 3–4 minutes or until it becomes deep red and develops a rich aroma. Return vegetables to pan. Add wine, stock, coffee and Worcestershire sauce. Cover and cook over a low heat, stirring occasionally, for 20 minutes.

4. Stir in oysters, parsley and cornstarch mixture. Cook, stirring, for 2–3 minutes or until mixture thickens. Remove pan from heat and allow to cool.

5. Preheat oven to 375°F/190°C. Transfer meat mixture to a deep pie dish. Roll out pastry and place over meat mixture. Bake for 20 minutes or until pastry is golden. Alternatively, bake in individual pie dishes. Serve with a green salad and crusty bread.

Serves 6

INDEX

INDEX

FAVORITES

FAVORITES

FAVORITES

FAVORITES

FAVORITES